ZENITH TRANS
RADIOS

Evolution of a Classic

Norman R. Smith

Schiffer Publishing Ltd

4880 Lower Valley Rd. Atglen, PA 19310 USA

DESIGNED BY BONNIE M. HENSLEY

ISBN: 0-7643-0015-6
Printed in the United States of America

Published by Schiffer Publishing Ltd.
4880 Lower Valley Road
Atglen, PA 19310
Phone: (610) 593-1777; Fax: (610) 593-2002
E-mail: Schifferbk@aol.com
Please write for a free catalog.
This book may be purchased from the publisher.
Please include $3.95 for shipping.

Please try your bookstore first.

We are interested in hearing from authors
with book ideas on related subjects.

DEDICATION

This book is dedicated to the memory of Jack Gordon Wright, who started me on my journey through the wondrous world of radio, to Mr. Elton Koops, my teacher, who was there with friendship and guidance when I really needed it and is still a good friend after thirty-seven years, and, of course, to all of the fine people at Zenith, past and present, who designed, manufactured, and marketed all of those great radios!

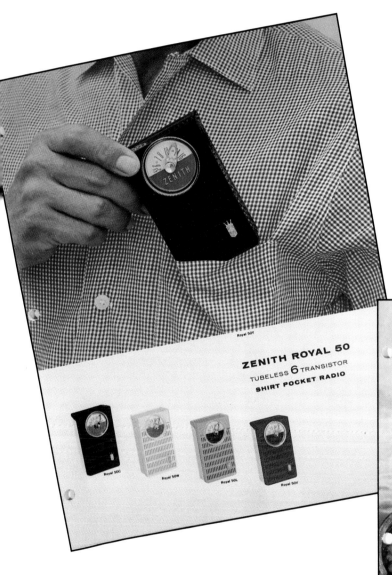

ACKNOWLEDGMENTS

As much as it has been a pleasure and an honor for me to write this book, it wouldn't have been possible for me to do so without the help of many others. Most of all, I would like to thank my wife, Sue, who puts up with my life in radio and all of its trappings.

I would also like to thank Susan Franko, my "Girl Friday," who put my ramblings into the computer and corrected much of my errant thought patterns, Bill Wade, a true friend who put me on to this project and contributed much information for its success, and John Taylor and Aimee Huntsha at Zenith Electronics Corporation, along with their entire staff. These people put up with me for two long years, and always came through for me when I needed their help. Many thanks to my friend and fellow radio collector, Karl Ayer, who went with me to Zenith in order to research the records and make photos and copies of them, as well as to help me interview Zenith employees. I also owe a debt of gratitude to the following present and former employees of Zenith, who shared with me much of the information needed to write this book: Rick Althans, Fran Greb, Howard Robins, and Bill Cheely. Special thanks to the Zenith Military Division people, Donn Abbot, Don Anderson, Bill Van Slyck, Bill Counts, Ralph Clarke, Jim Clark, and Clarence Pipes.

Sue and Fred

CONTENTS

INTRODUCTION

I was born at a time when radio was going through many changes. Television had taken over as a major source of news and family entertainment and radio was looking for a new identity to help it compete with TV. The radio industry saw a need to reinvent itself and found the answer by playing music. As "Rock and Roll" and "Country Music" came into the forefront of American culture, radio once again found a strong place in everyday life. Along with new programming came a revolution in radio technology. This revolution was created by the invention of the transistor in 1947. By the late 1950s, the transistor radio had changed the way we listened to radio: it was now possible to listen to the radio wherever, and whenever, you wanted to.

I was bitten by the radio bug at the early age of eight. I had heard the radio all of my life before that, but paid very little attention to it. Then, at eight years old, I received my first radio. It was an inexpensive crystal radio, but it opened up a whole new world for me. I could only pick up one or two local stations during the day, and most nights I could not receive anything. I lived near Grand Rapids, Michigan, and radio reception was difficult in that area. The real magic that captivated me happened late on some nights, when my radio helped transport me to far-off places like Chicago, or even Waterloo, Iowa. The receipt of such long distance signals instilled in me a life-long desire to travel the air waves to faraway places.

When I was eleven I received my first real radio. It was a Zenith model 4G800 tube portable. My stepfather was an amateur radio operator, and he bought the Zenith for me at a friend's moving sale. This radio was a quantum leap in performance from my earlier set. Hundreds of stations filled the Zenith's dial nearly every night, and this set even had a real speaker and volume control. Gone were the days of straining to hear those faint signals from afar. The little Zenith could take me to KFI in Los Angeles, KOA in Denver, KSL in Salt Lake City, WBZ in Boston, WABC in New York, and hundreds of other stations at night. It was now possible for me to listen to Chicago and Milwaukee—even during the day! My everyday friends were the Dee Jays at the "Big 89," WLS in Chicago. Ron Riley, Gene Taylor, Dick Biondi, and Art Roberts were my constant companions and they all played great music. I also listened to other great Dee Jays from all over the country. Over the next few years I owned a couple of small transistor radios, but none performed nearly as well as the little Zenith.

1961 was the year that I discovered high performance radios. A good friend of mine owned an Emerson model 888 "Vanguard" transistor portable. During the summer of 1961 it was stolen, and my friend's dad promptly bought him a new set. The new set was a Zenith Royal 500H. The sound that came from that small transistor radio was unbelievable! Along with its great sound, this set could pick up stations that I had never heard before. I immediately started saving my money so that I could also own one of these wondrous radios. The price was $59.95, quite a large sum of money for a fifteen-year-old to put together. I mowed lawns, delivered groceries, and later in the year shoveled snow to earn money for the Zenith. Christmas vacation of 1961 provided lots of snow, and therefore lots of work shoveling it. On January 4, 1962, I finally purchased the Royal 500H. The man at the radio store must have been glad to sell it to me—for months I had made my weekly trip to his store in order to try out the demo model. By the time I was finally ready to purchase the set, he knew me well. I insisted on buying the demo model because I knew it worked perfectly. I am sure he was glad to see it leave with me! I still have, and use, that radio today, and still haven't found a better performing small radio. The long distance listening hobby is also still with me, and when I am looking for those really hard to get stations the Royal 500H remains my radio of choice.

Over the years I have been the owner and collector of many Zenith radios, and I have learned to appreciate the quality and performance of these sets. The Zenith tradition of high performance quality radios was properly maintained and enhanced by these wonderful sets. Even today the Zenith name is respected and known to be representative of quality products. Zenith no longer makes radios, but they are an industry leader in television and many specialized products.

This book has been a labor of love for me and it has been a privilege to write it. The material for the book has been assembled over the last twenty years and the book itself took more time to put together than I ever thought it would. Finding and assembling the information was a major project. Even though I had the unlimited cooperation of the Zenith Electronics Corporation, there were many pieces of the puzzle missing. Many of the original records no longer exist, and memories have faded over the years. I searched all over the country for original Zenith photos and information. Thanks to the Zenith Electronics Corporation, many Zenith dealers, and fellow collectors, it was possible to come up with original photos of nearly all models made during those "magic" years at Zenith.

This book covers in detail the years 1955 through 1965, the years when major new advances in transistor radio technology were introduced. The early years produced many interesting and beautiful new models; many of these radios were to be the best ever produced. Changes in world economics finally brought an end to improvements in the field, and these aspects will also be covered.

Because Zenith led the industry and was so successful at marketing these radios, they were soon copied by other manufacturers and marketing organizations. If imitation is the sincerest form of flattery, the Zenith Radio Corporation should have been very flattered by the many ways their products were cloned by others.

Comments made throughout this book concerning the performance, quality of construction, and features utilized on various models are all in the opinion of the author. These opinions are based on many years of experience comparing radios for long distance reception as well as many years as a servicing technician.

Sit back, relax, and enjoy a trip back to the time when Zenith produced those fabulous radios, in *Zenith Transistor Radios, Evolution Of A Classic*.

Chapter 1

TRANSITIONS

Hearing Aids

Featured in the 1953 Zenith
Annual Report to stock-
holders.

Zenith's 10 year crusade to lower the cost of hearing has won the company an incalculable measure of good will, and has helped increase the growing acceptance of all Zenith products.

The crusade was launched on a stormy, rainy Sunday in October, 1943, with ads in Chicago papers. In spite of the bad weather 703 people came, to jam the sales room or to stand in rain drenched lines and wait for a chance to get in. Although there had been no advance notice and all sales were for cash, 83 people had the money ready that wet Sunday morning to buy a Zenith. Hundreds more were sold the next week.

Introduction of the new Zenith in other major markets was equally successful. Within months, this efficient, economical instrument brought help to thousands who could not afford the high prices asked for other makes.

Even though Zenith hearing aids have always sold for much less than other leading makes, their quality has never been surpassed. Zenith's low price was made possible by eliminating the enormous costs of high pressure selling.

Through the years Zenith hearing aids have blazed a brilliant trail of accomplishment and service to the public. Succeeding models have shown steady reduction in size while improving in per-

formance. The operating cost of Zenith hearing aids has averaged far less than competing instruments of comparable performance.

For these reasons, the Zenith has become the largest selling hearing aid in America.

In 1953 we introduced the tubeless all-transistor Royal-T, which we believe to be the finest hearing aid ever manufactured. Its battery cost of 15¢ per month is lower than any competing instrument of equivalent power, and a tiny fraction of the $4.50 to $9.00 per month for vacuum tube models.

The Royal-T has built public demand for Zenith hearing aids to an all-time high, substantially increasing your Company's margin of leadership in the hearing aid field.

Since demand continues for our vacuum tube models we have kept these in the line.

In the past year Zenith has conducted a highly successful advertising campaign aimed at overcoming the reluctance of many hard of hearing people to wear aids. One of our advertisements received several awards for merit and public service, and was read into the Congressional Record with favorable comment.

Only 15% of the hard of hearing people wear hearing aids today; we are making excellent progress with the 85% who do not.

1943-1953 *A Decade of Progress and Achievement in Providing Better Hearing at Lower Cost*

With the close of World War II in 1945, the United States was left as the strongest industrial force on earth. After suffering first the hardships of the depression, and then the problems accompanying a long major war, US citizens were once again ready to enjoy the fruits of their labor.

The returning soldiers were motivated to rejoin the work force and the industrial corporations were ready to convert back to manufacturing consumer products.

One of the big developments during the war was the miniaturization of electronic products. In order to make the most of limited space and power availability, major advances had been accomplished in this field during the war years.

In 1947, a team of AT&T scientists and engineers under the direction of William Shockley, Walter Bratten, and John Bardeen, made a major advance in the field of electronics. Their invention was called the transistor, and little did they know just how much it would change the future of so many technologies. The original purpose for its invention was to allow for in-line amplification of telephone circuits in order to improve long distance line communications. It was not until several years later that transistor technology advanced to the point where transistors could be used at the higher frequencies needed for radio.

Zenith Radio Corporation had started making hearing aids in October 1943. Zenith's Founder-President, Commander Eugene F. McDonald Jr., was partially deaf in one ear and recognized the need for affordable hearing aids; he therefore promoted Zenith's work in "Radionics." Hearing aids were the only civilian products produced by Zenith during World War II. This experience in miniaturization would serve them well in later years. Zenith's careful attention to quality and continuing improvements in performance placed them in a very competitive position in the hearing aid industry.

In October 1953 Zenith introduced its first fully transistorized hearing aid unit, the Royal T. This was a three transis-

FEATURES OF THE *Royal-T* ®

Greater Clarity...Greater Hearing Help
Zenith's transistors bring greater clarity than vacuum-tubes, and you enjoy the brilliant reception of an amazing new, super-sensitive microphone!

Greater Economy
The "Royal-T" operates for about 15¢ a month as compared to $4.50 to $9.00 per month for vacuum-tube aids of comparable power.

Greater Convenience
One 15¢ "A" battery operates the entire aid for a full month. No "B" battery, fewer interruptions in power, fewer battery changes.

4-Position Tone Control
Select high, medium, low or full range of tones covered by the instrument—whichever you need, wherever you go!

Fingertip Volume Control
So simple, so handy . . . afford instant variation of the volume you desire under all conditions.

New, More-Efficient Phonemagnet
Now clearer-than-ever, Zenith's built-in Phonemag- .... without air-borne sounds or interference.

Tiny External Microphone
Smartly-styled accessory for necktie, lapel, dress or suit . . . brings better hearing because of lessened clothing "whispers". Optional at small added cost.

e Tubeless, 3-Transistor *Royal-T*

, lightweight, easy to wear and to use, the superb new ith "Royal-T" is America's most-wanted hearing aid. It vastly dens the horizon of help that can be given to the hard-earing . . . sets a new high standard of performance, con- ence and economy.

ra-Powerful SUPER ROYAL-T ®
gned for those with very severe impair- ts. Same fine features, same small case same low price as the "Royal-T", but ewhat higher operating cost due to its ter power.

ZENITH'S OUTSTANDING VACUUM-TUBE INSTRUMENTS
◀ Extra-Small Royal ®
Extra-Powerful Super Royal ® ▶

ALITY RADIONICS Exclusively

FOR RELEASE Tuesday, November 22, 1955

Zenith Radio Corporation today announced the "Royal 500 all-transistor portable radio." This new portable radio uses seven transistors and weighs only 19 ounces, yet it is so powerful that it brings in weak, long distant stations which are ordinarily out of the range of 4-transistor miniature radios.

In announcing Zenith's first 7-transistor radio to the company's distributors, L. C. Truesdell, vice-president and director of sales, stated that the battery cost for the Royal 500 is much lower than for the average set of this type. The Zenith set operates for approximately 1¢ per hour as compared to 6 to 17¢ an hour for small, compact vacuum tube portables.

The power source for this set is four, tiny penlite batteries that are readily available in many stores for ten cents apiece, he said. The batteries can easily be replaced in a matter of seconds.

Truesdell explained that the Zenith Royal 500 has an unusual amount of power output. "As a means of comparison, this new set has 100 milliwatts of undistorted power output compared to six to twelve milliwatts of undistorted power output in the usual 4-transistor instruments, and the unusually sensitive circuitry in the new Zenith portable is the result of the company's experience in building hearing aids that use transistors as a replacement for vacuum tubes," he said. "The new circuitry," he added, "accomplishes previously unheard of economy and takes full advantage of the improved performance that transistors provide." Zenith is the largest user

page two continued on next page:

of transistors in the United States with the one exception of the telephone company.

The Royal 500, which is 3-1/2" wide; 5-3/4" high and 1-1/2" deep, has a non-breakable case of nylon material that withstands severe impact, Truesdell stated. A convenient 3-position handle swings above the cabinet for "carry about" use; slides down and back of the radio to serve as a table support; or hugs the bottom of the cabinet when the set is tucked into purse or pocket.

The dial is clearly marked with Civilian Defense frequencies. Also the set has a socket for a handy earphone attachment, optional at slight extra cost, which plugs into the set for private radio listening and cuts off the regular speaker, Truesdell said.

Cabinetry is black or maroon color with a gold-colored trim. Suggested retail price of the receiver, Truesdell said, is $75.00, less batteries.

- 30 -

Zenith Radio Corporation
6001 West Dickens Avenue
Chicago 39, Illinois
Tel: Berkshire 7-7500

111455

tor hearing aid, powered by a single 1 1/2 volt "N" cell battery. This unit operated at the cost of about 15 cents a month, while comparable vacuum tube models operated at a cost of between $4.50 and $9.00 a month.

As a result of their great success with the transistorized hearing aids, Zenith gained a rich experience in transistor technology. They soon expanded the hearing aid line to five different transistorized models in 1954 and continued to improve the performance of these products.

On November 22, 1955 the Zenith Radio Corporation released its first transistor radio, the Royal 500. This was the birth of the most successful transistor radio ever marketed. This event happened fully one year after the introduction of the world's first mass produced transistor radio, the Regency model TR-1. During 1955, many radio companies followed Regency's lead and introduced their own models. The unit introduced by Zenith, however, was not a follower, but a leader!

Chapter 2

BIRTH OF A LEGEND

There were many factors that made the Royal 500 a legendary performer.

Zenith, with the Royal 500, led the way in quality of construction and outstanding performance for transistor radios. The company designed and fabricated its own intermediate frequency (IF) and radio frequency (RF) transformers to exacting specifications of their own exclusive design. The outstanding sensitivity and selectivity of these radios give testimony to their excellent engineering, driven by the flamboyant leader, Commander McDonald. The audio frequency transformers were also done in-house, and again provided exceptional performance. Most other manufacturers relied on general suppliers for their transformers; the efficiency of such transformers was not very good because they needed to operate with a variety of circuit designs, and most sets using them lacked high performance characteristics.

Original Royal 500, released November 1955.

ZENITH ROYAL "500"
Tubeless
7 TRANSISTOR
Pocket Radio

The Royal 500 was equipped with seven plug-in transistors on a hand-wired metal chassis, 7XT40, which produced a full 100 milliwatts of undistorted audio output. Utilizing a 2-3/4 inch speaker, this radio had outstanding tonal qualities, thanks to Zenith's experience with acoustic engineering in both radio and hearing aid development. The transistors were supplied by Texas Instruments, Sylvania, and Raytheon. Powered by four "AA" pen-lite batteries, the Royal 500 also had greater sensitivity than most comparably sized radios. The radio's exceptional ability to receive signals under adverse conditions, such as in a shielded building or in a train or automobile, gave it wide acceptance as a powerful performer. Zenith also paid close attention to the physical appearance of their star performer. The use of unbreakable nylon for the cabinet was an expensive but excellent choice of material. This beautiful cabinet, available in either black or maroon and accented with gold metal trim, made a truly elegant appearing radio. Some early examples of this radio feature a translucent maroon cabinet which allows one to see inside the set under certain lighting conditions. Another Zenith innovation was the 3-position swing handle, which allowed the set to be carried by the handle, supported it in a lean-back position, or folded down to the bottom for convenient placement of the radio in pocket or purse. The dimensions of the set were 3-1/2 inches wide by 5-3/4 inches high by 1-1/2 inches deep. The radio weighed in at a mere nineteen ounces. The original Royal 500 sold for $75.00, expensive in its day but a real value for the transistor radio enthusiast demanding the best in the industry.

ASSEMBLY OF FAMOUS ROYAL "500" pocket radio requires the finest of precision workmanship. Shown is assembly point where chassis receives seven tiny transistors.

IN SCREEN ROOM tests, Royal "500" pocket radio must meet sensitivity, gain, and battery drain requirements which have made it industry's performance leader.

From Annual Report of 1956.

Chapter 3

1956

The year 1956 brought with it many changes at Zenith, including the pioneering introduction of "Space Command," the world's first practical wireless TV remote control. Yet few changes were made that year in the Zenith line-up of transistor radios. The Royal 500 circuitry was revised three times to further improve its performance. Early production Royal 500s contained chassis 7XT40 with circuit one or circuit two variations. Later series contained the 7XT40Z or 7XT40Z1 chassis. At a time when transistor radios from most other manufacturers were able to receive only strong local stations, the Zenith Royal 500 was a hot performer with excellent audio as well. Although it was priced at $75.00, sales of the Royal 500 skyrocketed far beyond Zenith's expectations.

Zenith introduced a larger transistor portable in 1956. The Royal 800 shared some styling characteristics with the Royal 500. This lunch-box-sized portable weighed four pounds, four ounces with its complement of eight "C" sized batteries. It employed a 4 inch speaker and put out an amazing 500 milliwatts of undistorted audio. This seven transistor set, chassis 7ZT41, was an exceptionally sensitive receiver for its time and was the only Zenith radio to come equipped with GE "top hat" style transistors. The Wave Magnet antenna was located in a pop-up handle. This was of questionable engineering because when the operator carried the radio by its handle, the efficiency of the antenna coil would be altered and performance would suffer. Similar style radios from Motorola, Admiral, Emerson, and Philco were plagued by this same problem. Fortunately, Zenith did not repeat this mistake very often: the Royal 755LF, Royal 790Y, and 790YK were the only other Zeniths of this design.

The Royal 800 was available in either ebony or a two-tone silver gray with gobelin blue nylon cabinet, accented with a beautiful large gold speaker grille. The Royal 800 sold for $89.50.

Zenith Tubeless **7** Transistor Portable Radio

ROYAL "800Y"

Ebony

Also available as Royal "800G"
in Silver Gray and Gobelin Blue

Zenith's second transistor radio, the Royal 800; released December 1955.

Chapter 4
1957

1957 was an exciting year at Zenith. The great success enjoyed by the Royal 500 led Commander McDonald to direct his engineers in developing a greatly expanded line-up of transistor portables. The new flagship of the transistor line was the brand new "all-transistor Trans-Oceanic" portable radio. This set was first introduced as the transistor "Trans-Oceanic" and carried no Royal designation. It was later given the Royal 1000 name.

From Annual Report of 1957.

Zenith Radio Corporation

CHICAGO

TED LEITZELL
DIRECTOR
PUBLIC RELATIONS

November 1, 1957

TO ALL ZENITH DISTRIBUTORS:

Here - for your use and advantage - is press material on the new all-transistor Trans-Oceanic portable.

Each press release and pic is sent to you in quadruplicate. The releases are planned for different editors -- i.e., the general announcement story goes to financial editors of newspapers; the semi-technical story to science editors. The marine uses of the set are in another story, designed for yachting editors, if you are located in an area where there is recreational boating.

Appropriate pics are available for each story. The outline print is for shopping column use now; the Christmas "shot" for columns during the pre-holiday shopping season.

If you need additional pics and releases, let me know. They'll be back to you fast.

We ask you to exert every effort in placing this publicity with the newspapers and magazines published in your territory.

The Trans-Oceanic is far and away the most versatile receiver Zenith has ever built. It is a prestige gift item and a reliable, high-efficiency performer. Markets for the set include executives in commerce and industry; members of the professions; outdoorsmen of all interests; groups of foreign language speaking peoples in the U. S., etc. etc.

At Zenith, our people have begun an intensive program of pre-selling these users by direct mail. The enclosed press material offers you the opportunity to pre-sell the Trans-Oceanic by publicity in your sales area where it cannot help but benefit you and your organization.

As you have done in the past, please supply me with clips of every story you place.

Many thanks. Good luck.

Cordially,

Ted Leitzell

TL:j
Att.

Zenith letter to distributors regarding "Trans-Oceanic."

FOR RELEASE TUESDAY, NOVEMBER 5, 1957

#1.

WORLD'S FIRST ALL-TRANSISTOR
BAND-SPREAD SHORT WAVE PORTABLE
INTRODUCED BY ZENITH

Chicago, Nov. 5 -- Zenith Radio Corporation today introduced what company officials describe as the most magnificent radio receiver ever built. It is the new all-transistor Trans-Oceanic* portable, world's first all-transistor set with band-spread short wave tuning.

Announcement was made by L. C. Truesdell, Zenith vice-president and director of sales.

The new receiver tunes eight wave bands to give magnificent reception from thousands of foreign stations on international short wave channels, plus super-sensitive reception of ship-to-shore communications, Coast Guard weather broadcasts and standard broadcast stations. Truesdell said that band-spread tuning on international short wave bands electronically stretches the distance between stations on the dial to permit precision selection of even weak or far-distant short wave stations.

*Reg. U.S. Pat. Off.

Press Release, November 5, 1957 regarding "Trans-Oceanic."

continued on next page

Because of its extreme sensitivity, selectivity and range of reception, he said, the Trans-Oceanic supplies the tourist, traveler, sportsman and sailor with everything he needs by radio for his greater "away-from-home" enjoyment and safety.

Truesdell said that the set is a precision instrument, housed in a gleaming chrome-plated cabinet trimmed in black leather and designed by Mel Boldt, one of the nation's foremost industrial designers. It is the size of an ordinary portable, he stated, and is by far the smallest and lightest band-spread short wave portable ever produced. Weight, 13 pounds including batteries, is half that of conventional short wave portables.

The new Trans-Oceanic is engineered to perform efficiently on trains, planes, boats, automobiles, in steel buildings - where portable radio failure is common - and in extremes of climate from the frozen Arctic to steaming equatorial jungles, he said.

The set is powered by ordinary flashlight batteries, available anywhere in the world, and will operate up to three hundred hours on a set, to give a cost of about half a cent per hour at ordinary volume, Truesdell said. This efficient transistor operation eliminates need for tubes, high cost "B" batteries, or electric power line connection.

Zenith engineers rate the receiver at 500 milliwatts of undistorted power output, 92% greater than for any tube type short wave portable, which gives exceptional tone quality.

(More)

1.

continued on next page

- 3 -

Truesdell said the receiver is a companion model to Zenith's world-famed vacuum tube Trans-Oceanic that has been supreme in the short wave portable field in American and overseas markets since the original Trans-Oceanic was introduced in 1941. No single model receiver in radio's history, he said, has achieved the world-wide reputation for service which the Trans-Oceanic enjoys.

"More than three years of intensive research, engineering and field testing," he said, "have gone into the transistorized Trans-Oceanic." He disclosed that the engineering and tooling investment amounted to approximately $300,000.

There are three antennas: the telescoping Waverod, exclusively for short wave use, which is built into the handle; the built-in Wavemagnet* antenna for normal reception of standard broadcasts; and the detachable Wavemagnet that increases sensitivity up to 300 per cent in trains, planes, automobiles, etc.

Front cover of the set houses a comprehensive set of log charts, listing weather broadcast schedules for the Great Lakes, Pacific and Atlantic coastal areas, the Gulf of Mexico and Caribbean Sea areas and U.S. river navigation. Also listed are all major short wave stations of the world, with frequencies and times of best reception, including the Voice of America, United Nations and Armed Forces radio stations.

Other features include: a time zone dial and world time zone map - etched in metal; an earphone connection for "private listening" purposes; a phonograph jack that permits any record player with a high output cartridge to be used with the set; a dialite for

*Reg. U.S. Pat. Off.   (More)

1.
____

continued on next page

night-time tuning, and separate volume and tone controls.

In appearance, Truesdell said, the set has the precision look of the finest camera. It is 10¼" high (including the
handle); 12½" wide and 4-7/8" deep.

Suggested retail price is $250, which includes
batteries - 8 for the set and one for the dialite.

- 30 -

Zenith Radio Corporation
6001 W. Dickens
Chicago 39, Illinois

1.

The overall attention to quality in every detail of this radio exemplifies Zenith's long standing commitment to McDonald's vision of "Quality Without Compromise." This hand-wired, nine transistor multi-band radio, chassis 9AT40, is encased in a beautiful black leather and brushed aluminum cabinet accented with real chrome trim. The set weights in at thirteen pounds, including the nine "D" cell batteries which power it. The eight different wave bands give excellent performance across the spectrum. This set was truly a major advance in performance for transistor radio technology, and is still an exceptional performer, even by current standards. The Royal 1000 "Trans-Oceanic" remained basically unchanged through 1957.

Sold for $250.00, the Royal 1000 still enjoyed good sales due to its exceptional performance.

The Royal 500 was improved again in 1957. The biggest change was the use of a printed circuit board in place of the hand-wired metal chassis. This set still carried a complement of seven transistors which were supplied by Sylvania, Texas Instruments, or Raytheon. There were many circuit changes which greatly improved performance. The new Royal 500 employed a vernier tuning capacitor; in conjunction with the newly redesigned knobs this capacitor made tuning stations much easier. "On/off" and volume were also easier to control with the new knob design. Sensitivity and selectivity were improved with revised

RF circuit designs. Zenith also expanded the choice of cabinet colors to include ebony, white, maroon, pink, or beige. The pink and beige models were produced in limited quantities and are quite rare today. The Royal 500 for 1957 used the 7ZT40 and 7ZT40Z1 chassis and sold for $75.00.

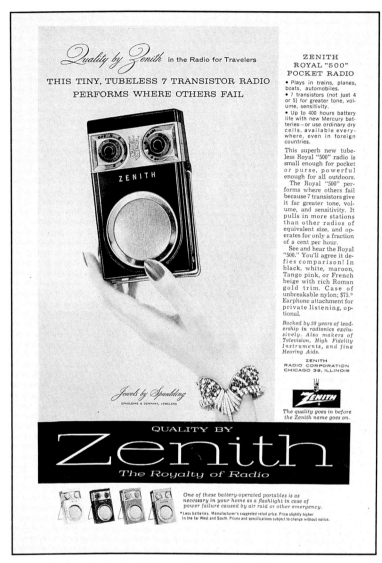

Advertisement in *National Geographic* magazine, July 1957.

Zenith factory spec sheet photo, Royal 700.

In order to capture a larger segment of the transistor radio market, Zenith also introduced several other major new models in 1957.

The Royal 700 was a leather encased portable which took the place of the Royal 800. This seven transistor set, chassis 7AT43, was more compact and had a more durable cabinet design than the Royal 800. It was available in a black or brown cowhide cabinet accented with a large die cast metal speaker grille. It still carried the 4 inch speaker and had excellent tone and volume. This set put out 275 milliwatts of clean audio. The radio was powered by a complement of six "C" cell batteries, and it retailed for $69.95.

Zenith also introduced the all new Royal 750 in 1957. This leather portable radio was an exceptionally strong performer. It enjoyed a complement of eight transistors (supplied by RCA) on chassis 8AT41, and used a three gang tuning capacitor and a tuned RF amplifier circuit. This radio set the standard by which to judge the performance of all other lunch-box-sized portables. Its exceptional sensitivity made it a real joy to use when trying to pick up those weak long distance stations that are hard to receive. This high performance portable contained a 4 inch speaker driven by a 275 milliwatt audio amplifier with plenty of reserve power and excellent tonal characteristics. The radio used six "C" cell batteries and operated for many hours on a single set. It was available in tan or black genuine cowhide, accented by a gold-tone speaker grille assembly. The Royal 750 was priced at $79.95.

ZENITH ROYAL 750
TUBELESS 8 TRANSISTOR
PORTABLE RADIO
GENUINE LEATHER CABINET

Zenith factory spec sheet photo, Royal 750.

Another new addition to the 1957 line was the Royal 300. This radio contained a complement of seven transistors and had nearly identical circuitry to the earlier Royal 500 chassis 7ZT40. The Royal 300 chassis designation was 7AT42. This set had one of the most attractive nylon cabinets of all the Zenith portables. The designers even thought of small improvements such as the three small feet which project slightly out from the back of this radio, enabling it to lie down without scratching the back. This feature also improved tonal response when the radio was in the lie-back position. This cabinet also featured the familiar 3-way handle design first introduced with the Royal 500. The Royal 300 was produced in ebony, maroon, and pine frost green. A few were also made in white. It sold for $59.95.

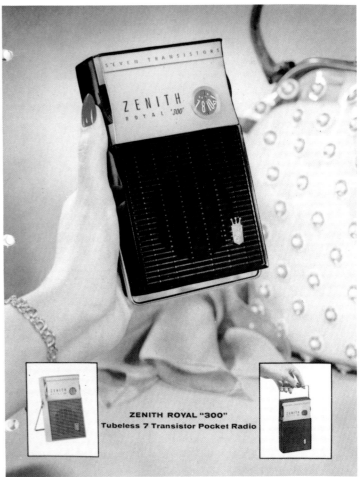

ZENITH ROYAL "300"
Tubeless 7 Transistor Pocket Radio

Zenith factory spec sheet photo, Royal 300.

Making the best better

ZENITH'S ROYAL 500D

World's most powerful radio of its size!

In 1955, Zenith introduced an all-transistor pocket radio that defied comparison—The Royal 500. It was the world's most powerful radio of its size, reflecting Zenith's lifelong policy not to compromise quality for price. Within a few months, the Royal 500 became the standard of excellence and performance in the industry. To make the best even better, Zenith, in 1957, added an untuned RF stage which increased signal sensitivity *four* times! Now, in 1959, Zenith's unique new inverted cone speaker gives the Royal 500D a richness of tone never before possible in so small a radio.

Making the best better is no new consideration at Zenith. For over 40 years, Zenith has maintained two policy principles regarding quality manufacture. First, to develop and produce products of the highest quality. Second, and no less important, to strive constantly to improve products even though they rate best with millions. That's why consumers have learned to respect such features as the Zenith long distance radio chassis, the handsome, acoustically designed cabinets, the exclusive Wavemagnet® antenna that brings in even distant signals sharp and clear.

And Zenith is determined to continue making the best better; to continue making Quality a way of life; to continue applying the most stringent standards in the industry to all Zenith products.

This is our way of giving you, the Zenith dealer, not only more sales, but something more to sell than a price tag.

Commander McDonald died in 1958, but the spirit of innovation he led at Zenith lived on. 1958 brought another major revision to the Royal 500 design. The radio was now designated as the Royal 500D and was the first of the high performance Royal 500s. The set carried a complement of eight transistors with the addition of a new broadband radio frequency amplifier circuit, and further improved intermediate frequency amplifier circuits. RCA supplied the transistors for all Zenith transistor portables built from 1958 through 1963. Most Zenith models were equipped with plug-in transistors, a feature that allowed for easy repair of a radio with transistor problems.

In an effort to improve tonal presence in a small radio, Zenith had begun a program of experimental speaker design. The Royal 500D was the first radio to receive one of the new speakers. Zenith used an inverted cone design in order to get more volume and improved tone from this set. Not all Royal 500D radios had the inverted cone speaker, and only later production models have the 500D painted on the front of the radio. The chassis designation of the Royal 500D is 8AT40Z2.

The Royal 500D was produced in ebony, white, and maroon cabinet colors. The speaker grille area was redesigned to accommodate the new speaker. A radio equipped with a concave designed speaker grille always contained a speaker with the normal configuration. Radios equipped with a convex designed speaker grille may contain either the normal or the reverse cone speaker. The volume knob was also given the addition of a clear plastic skirt to match the dial scale knob. The retail price for the Royal 500D remained $75.00.

The 1958 line-up of radios was expanded significantly in response to great consumer interest in transistor radios. The Royal 1000 "Trans-Oceanic" was joined by the Royal 1000D. This set was released with the addition of a long wave navigation band along with the eight bands already covered by the Royal 1000. Both were marketed at the same time and the Royal 1000, chassis 9AT40, sold for $250.00 while the Royal 1000D, chassis 9AT41Z2, retailed at $275.00. For detailed information on the Trans-Oceanic line, please refer to *The Zenith Trans-Oceanic: The Royalty of Radios* by John H. Bryant, AIA and Harold N. Cones, Ph.D. This book is available through Schiffer Publishing.

Zenith factory spec sheet photo, Royal 500D.

Zenith factory spec sheet photo, Royal 1000 "Trans-Oceanic."

Previous page:
Zenith Royal 500D advertisement as it appeared in *Electrical Merchandising,* May 1959.

Another Zenith release in 1958 was the Royal 200, an oversized vertical design transistor set which looked as though it were designed much earlier. This set was similar in size to the Emerson model 888 series of radios. Zenith used a plastic cabinet which was somewhat fragile and easily damaged. It came in four colors: brown, white, coral, and green. This seven transistor portable, chassis 7AT48, contained an oversized 3-1/2 inch speaker and was powered by four "AA" pen-lite batteries. The Royal 200 was an average performer and not up to Zenith's usual high performance standards. The painted on dial scale was difficult to read and very easily damaged. Also, the molded plastic cabinet was quite brittle and easily chipped or broken. Nice examples of this set are hard to find. The Royal 200 retailed at $44.95.

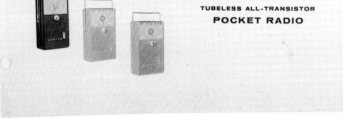

Zenith factory spec sheet photo, Royal 200.

The Royal 450 was a radically new design for Zenith. This was an oversized pocket radio built with a horizontally oriented design. This seven transistor set, chassis 7AT45Z1, was a better than average performer with exceptional audio performance for its size. The cabinet came in three colors: ebony, white, or orange. The plastic cabinet, although quite attractive, was easily broken if the set

was dropped or knocked over. This radio is a very rare model, as production was limited. The set was powered by six "AA" pen-lite cells and the leakage of these battery types also took its toll on many radios. The Royal 450 retailed at $59.95.

Zenith factory spec sheet photo, Royal 450.

A new series of sets appeared with the introduction of the Royal 760 "Navigator" radio. This set was very similar in external appearance to the Royal 750. Inside this super-powered portable was a hand-wired, weather resistant metal chassis, 8AT42, which received not only the standard broadcast band but also the long wave navigation band, 200-400 Khz. A tuned RF stage was employed to give this set amazing sensitivity. Precision vernier tuning made this an easy set to tune. A "Normal-Navigate" switch allows the Automatic Gain Control (AGC) circuit to be deactivated; as a result, it is easy to null-out a signal by rotating this set, making radio navigation much easier than with the AGC circuit engaged. Outstanding volume and tone were produced by the 4 inch speaker, which was driven by an amplifier capable of producing up to 275 milliwatts of audio output. Powered by six "C" sized cells, the Royal 760 could operate up to 350 hours on a set of batteries. The one bad feature found on this receiver was the location of the earphone jack. This was located on the inside of the back and required the operator to open the back in order to gain access to the jack, leading to problems with early fatigue of the hinge located on the upper back of this radio (the Royals 675, 700, 710, 750, and 755 all suffer from this same design problem). The genuine leather cabinet on the Royal 760 is a light tan color cowhide, and is accented by a beautiful die cast chrome-plated grille assembly. Considering the quality of construction and the outstanding performance of this radio, the Royal 760, priced at $99.95, was an exceptional value.

Zenith factory spec sheet photo, Royal 760 "Navigator."

A different direction for Zenith was the release of two new cordless clock radio designs. The Royal 850 was a portable clock radio, based on the chassis design of the Royal 200. The 7AT47 chassis used seven transistors and was identical to the Royal 200, except that it was turned on its side in a horizontal position and the Wave-Magnet antenna was relocated to accommodate this change. The set was an average performer but did enjoy the advantage of vernier tuning, unlike its Royal 200 counterpart. Available in four different colors—antique white, brown,

pink, or charcoal brown—all complemented with an antique white back, this set was quite attractive. The radio contained a four jewel imported electric clock assembly which would operate up to one year on a single "D" cell battery. The clock could control the on/off operation of the radio and allowed the user to wake to music wherever this cordless clock radio was used. The Royal 850 sold for the price of $85.00.

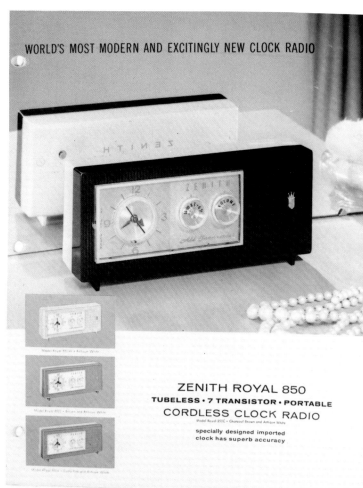

Zenith factory spec sheet photo, Royal 850.

An outstanding new entry in the 1958 line-up was the beautifully styled Zenith "Golden Triangle," presumably one of Commander McDonald's last directives in the design of transistor radios. The Royal 950 was one of the most unusual and elegant transistor radios ever produced. This radio was encased in a three-sided gold-finished cabinet set on a built-in swivel stand with three legs. This design allowed for easy rotation, which would expose any one of three different faces to the user. One face contains the control knobs and dial scale. The next face displays the seven jewel battery-operated Swiss clock and control lever. The third face contains the speaker grille bearing the Zenith logo. Each face is accented with a seventeen karat gold ring surrounding its features. The top and bottom of the cabinet are constructed of a charcoal gray acrylic material. A smartly styled handle accents the top of this set and allows for easy orientation. The seven transistor chassis, 7AT46, is based on the famous Royal 500 design. The battery compartment is identical in design to that of the Royal 500 and early production models contain a thin plastic half-back in order to cover the chassis components. This cover closely resembles a Royal 500 back. Similar in performance to the seven transistor Royal 500, the Royal 950 had better tone, thanks to its larger 3-1/2 inch speaker. Access to the battery compartments of both the radio and clock is gained by opening the radio control/dial scale face of the cabinet, which hinges open for easy entry. The radio operated on four "AA" pen-lite batteries and the clock was powered by a single "D" cell battery. This radio sold for $150.00 and was truly "The World's Most Elegant Clock Radio."

The 1958 line-up of new Zenith radios was an outstanding display of Zenith's careful attention to "Quality Without Compromise." These sets enjoyed unparalleled performance, and some models will still easily outperform even the best radios of the 1990s.

Right: Zenith factory spec sheet photo, Royal 950 "Golden Triangle."

Below: From Annual Report of 1958.

ZENITH *Golden Triangle* Royal 950

ALL-TRANSISTOR CORDLESS CLOCK RADIO

Specially designed Swiss clock has superb accuracy

7 TRANSISTORS · NO TUBES · NO CORDS

27

Capitalizing on its transistor radio expertise, Zenith expanded its hearing aid line-up in 1958 to include five different shirt pocket models and two behind-the-ear models. There were also three different eyeglass mounted models, and one of these operated on solar power!

THE ROYALTY OF HEARING AIDS

CREATIVELY DESIGNED TO RECAPTURE THE JOY OF LIVING SOUND

Zenith's crusade for better hearing made notable progress in 1958. The revision of our product line, highlighted by the introduction of several new models, improved dealer facilities, and the support of aggressive advertising and merchandising programs accounted for these gains.

Each of the eight new aids introduced during the year reflected the vast knowledge and experience gained in Zenith's 40 years of research in the fields of sound and hearing.

New models were skillfully designed and engineered to compensate for a variety of hearing impairments,

with accent on style, performance, and economy. These creative efforts produced a line of "Living Sound" hearing aids that offered more features, more pleasure, and greater economy in a variety of styles than ever before possible.

Each new model provides the outstanding performance and proven dependability that have consistently gained favor for Zenith with hearing aid users everywhere. And despite rising production costs, all were sensibly priced, consistent with Zenith's policy of bringing within the reach of all the highest quality hearing help possible.

THE DIPLOMAT®   THE AMBASSADOR

MODELS FOR EVERY TYPE OF ELECTRONICALLY CORRECTIBLE HEARING LOSS

THE DIPLOMAT—Now 30% smaller than former Diplomat, still it delivers full power with a brilliant 4-transistor circuit. Weighing only one-half ounce with battery, the new Diplomat with a miniature "Power Mite" earphone and fingertip controls, sets a new standard of at-the-ear wearing ease and convenience.

THE AMBASSADOR—This new instrument is unique in its class. Conducts sound to the ear through a plastic tube, eliminating the customary earphone in the ear. So small and light, it is easily worn at the ear. Delivers adequate power for all mild to moderate losses.

THE CREST®
Most versatile hearing aid built. Thanks to external microphone, it can actually be worn ten different ways.

THE CRUSADER
Small and compact, with superb tone and range. New "battery-saver" circuit. Exclusive Phone Magnet.

THE PREMIER
Brilliant styling, operating economy, and full power performance. Fingertip tone and volume controls.

THE ECONOMICAL 50-R
Specifically engineered and produced to bring top quality performance and true hearing pleasure within reach of all.

THE REGENT®
Miniature in size but super-powered, having many times the power of average aid. Ideal for the person with severe hearing loss.

ZENITH—40 YEARS OF LEADERSH

ZENITH EYEGLASS HEARING AIDS

Four brilliant new models introduced in 1958 enabled Zenith hearing aid dealers to competitively meet and satisfy the growing trend to eyeglass hearing aids. Hearing aid users, many of whom presently wear eyeglasses, have found a new sense of well-being and poise by combining eyeglass and hearing aid needs into one inconspicuous unit. The ease and convenience with which many could now enjoy the thrills of stereophonic sound with binaural or "both ear" hearing also contributed to the popularity of eyeglass hearing aids. Each of the new models is a true example of Zenith quality, offering the style, performance, and dependability users everywhere associate with the name Zenith.

THE CITATION—The ultimate in styling and performance for both men and women. This deluxe, 4-transistor model delivers superb performance and outstanding economy of operation with its "battery-saver" circuit. Slim, trim, "Custom Contoured" temple bars fit head snugly, rest lighter behind the ear. "Adjusto-Fit" feature permits instant interchange of sunglass, safety, or conventional eyeglass fronts. Available in a variety of attractive colors.

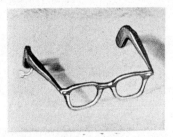

THE CHALLENGER
An economical, 3-transistor model. Adequate power for all with a mild or moderate hearing loss. Color-styled to suit the most discriminating user. Thanks to its low cost, the thrill of binaural hearing is now well within the budget of thousands.

THE SOLARIS
With its temple-mounted silicon solar cells, the Solaris not only operates on free sun power, but also stores reserve power in its battery when sufficient sun rays are available. When not in sunlight, it operates at full power on either a mercury or rechargeable nickel-cadmium battery.

THE IMPERIAL—High quality, dependable electronic hearing help, *with absolutely nothing in the ear*. For the thousands with impaired hearing who can use a bone conduction hearing aid, the Imperial provides outstanding performance features. Its exclusive, self-adjusting sound plate (see inset above) is swivel-mounted for full contact with the mastoid bone, assuring positive transmission of amplified sound to the hearing nerves in the inner ear. Richly-styled, distinctive black temple bars attractively blend or contrast with a variety of frame fronts.

QUALITY RADIONICS EXCLUSIVELY

Chapter 6

1959

1959 again brought the introduction of many new transistor models to the Zenith line, plus some existing models received an external "facelift" with the circuitry remaining unchanged.

The greatly redesigned Royal 500E received a much different look with a dramatically restyled cabinet. The overall dimensions and concept were not changed, but the nylon cabinet style and texture were much different than that used on earlier models. The upper one third of the cabinet was covered by a bright gold-plated control knob escutcheon, accented by larger knobs to control on/off, volume, and tuning functions. The larger knobs made control of this set much easier. This brightly finished piece was very attractive when new, but very vulnerable to damage due to its construction. It is almost impossible to find an undamaged example of this radio unless the radio was never used. Many were damaged the first time they were placed into the leather styled case, which was actually

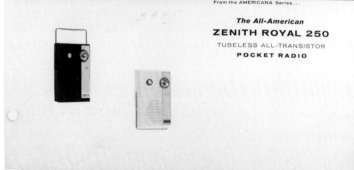

Zenith factory spec sheet photo, Royal 250.

Zenith factory spec sheet photo, Royal 500E.

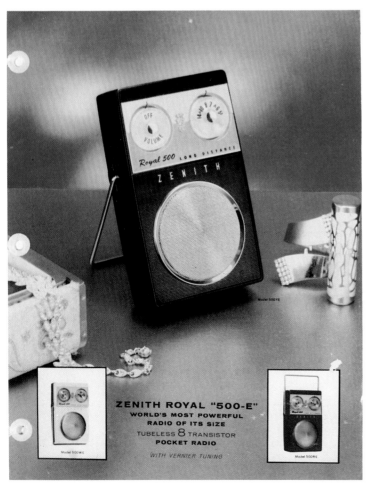

supposed to protect them. The inside snap of this case had bare metal which usually scraped the front of the Royal 500E and damaged it. Although one of very few Zenith design mistakes, this was definitely a time when a touch of extra thought was needed. The speaker grille was redesigned and came with either a smooth or textured finish. The radio was available in maroon, black, white, or a two-tone model with white front and brick red colored back. The two-toned set is relatively rare and the envy of transistor radio collectors today.

The circuitry for the Royal 500E's chassis 8CT40Z2 was nearly identical to the 8AT40Z2 chassis used on the Royal 500D. The Royal 500E was supplied with either the conventional speaker or the reverse cone speaker. When first introduced it sold for $75.00, but economic pressures created by ever increasing sales of imported models forced

Zenith to reduce the price to $59.95. This trend in pricing would lead to a dramatic change in transistor radio marketing practices.

To remain competitive with lower priced sets, Zenith expanded the choice of models based on the Royal 500 concept. The "All-American," Zenith Royal 250, was the low cost entry model and sold for $39.95. It contained chassis 6CT40Z1 and was a basic six transistor design with direct drive tuning. It was powered by four "AA" pen-lite batteries. A less expensive polystyrene cabinet was used and was available in black, white, or tan, each accented by gold trim.

The next step up was the Royal 275 "Statesman." Again, the less expensive polystyrene cabinet was employed and it came in four color choices. All of them were two-toned combinations: dark brown with a light tan back, dark blue with a light blue back, ebony with a beige back, and dark green with a light green back. The chassis, 7CT40Z1, was very similar in performance to the second series Royal 500. The Royal 275 sold for $49.95.

Zenith also made additions to the leather portable line-up. The Royal 675 "Independence" looked very similar to the more powerful Royal 750. The Royal 675, chassis 6CT41Z1, was a basic six transistor design with the addition of vernier tuning. This set displays unusually good sensitivity for a six transistor set. Excellent volume and tone were produced by the 200 milliwatt audio amplifier driving a 4 inch speaker. The Royal 675 was available in a reddish brown "Permawear" artificial leather cabinet, highlighted with an attractive chromium-plated speaker grille. The set was powered by four "C" sized cells. The Royal 675 sold for $49.95.

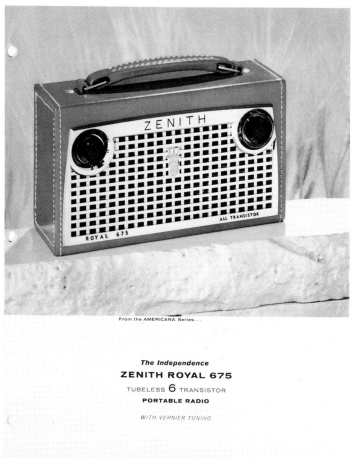

From the AMERICANA Series...

The Independence
ZENITH ROYAL 675
TUBELESS **6** TRANSISTOR
PORTABLE RADIO
WITH VERNIER TUNING

Zenith factory spec sheet photo, Royal 675.

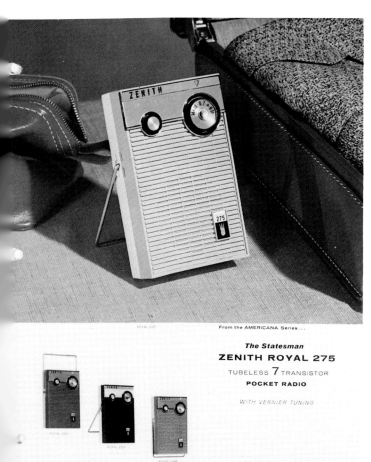

From the AMERICANA Series...

The Statesman
ZENITH ROYAL 275
TUBELESS **7** TRANSISTOR
POCKET RADIO
WITH VERNIER TUNING

Zenith factory spec sheet photo, Royal 275.

Later in 1959 Zenith released the Royal 710 "Yorktown" to take the place of the Royal 700. The seven transistor chassis 7CT43Z1 was very similar in design to the Royal 700, but the cabinet had been significantly restyled for a more modern look. The knobs were enlarged, which made tuning much easier. The cabinet was constructed of the less expensive "Permawear" material and came in a saddle brown color highlighted by an attractive chrome-plated grille. Some slight changes in circuitry gave the Royal 710 even better tonal performance than the Royal 700. The set sold for $59.95.

ZENITH ROYAL 710

TUBELESS 7 TRANSISTOR

PORTABLE RADIO

WITH VERNIER TUNING

Zenith factory spec sheet photo, Royal 710.

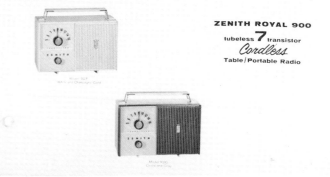

Zenith factory spec sheet photo, Royal 900.

One of the rarest of all Zenith transistor radios is the Royal 900. This seven transistor set, chassis 7AT44Z1, was designed to be a cordless table radio, which is probably the reason for its small production run. Powered by eight "C" size cells, this set put out an amazing 500 milliwatts of undistorted audio. Its 4 inch speaker produced outstanding volume and tone. This set was quite attractive and had a very unusual but nice looking dial scale. This set is a real find for the Zenith transistor radio collector. The Royal 900 sold for $69.95.

The Royal 750 was given an all new look and designated as the Royal 755. A greatly restyled die cast cabinet face now contained a slide rule dial and larger knobs than the original. The genuine top grain cowhide cabinet was available in a brown color. Some early production sets, chassis 8ET41Z2, were equipped with a large plastic handle which contained the antenna. This handle could be rotated in order to allow the directional antenna to be aimed for best reception, while still allowing the radio to be placed in the best position for listening. Although this feature sounds advantageous, it is overpowered by the adverse effect created by placing a hand on the radio's antenna-handle. Reception of weaker stations was degraded by this practice. Zenith soon realized the problems with this design and returned to installing the antenna inside the radio, where it performed better.

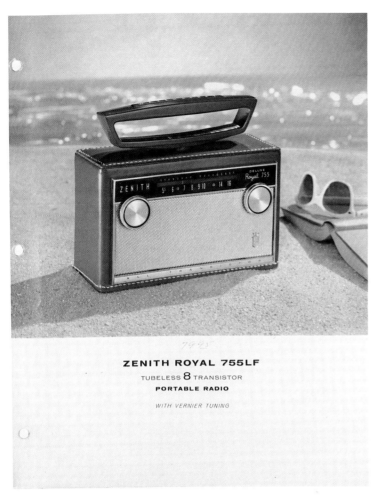

ZENITH ROYAL 755LF

TUBELESS 8 TRANSISTOR

PORTABLE RADIO

WITH VERNIER TUNING

ZENITH *Royal 780YG*

the **NAVIGATOR**

SUPER-SENSITIVE · TWO-BAND
TUBELESS · 8 TRANSISTOR
PORTABLE RADIO

Super-sensitive receiver tunes standard broadcast and government LF weather-navigation bands . . . ideal for fliers, yachtsmen, tourists, outdoorsmen . . . and all who need outstanding reception of broadcast stations plus up-to-the-hour weather reports, as well as long-range reception of favorite programs on standard broadcast stations at home . . . on the beach . . . or while traveling.

**SELF-POWERED, EMERGENCY, NAVIGATIONAL AID
FOR PLANES AND BOATS**

Zenith factory spec sheet photo, Royal 755.

Zenith factory spec sheet photo, Royal 780.

The Royal 760 "Navigator" was reincarnated as the Royal 780 with a similar facelift. One major improvement was the 1/4 inch phone jack mounted on the left side panel of the cabinet. The 8CT42Z2 chassis was still a hand-wired metal unit with a moisture resistant transformer design. The frequency coverages for the Royal 780 were the same as used on the Royal 760. The tuning and volume knobs were enlarged for easier operation. The band switch and Normal-Navigate knobs were redesigned and much stronger than the Royal 760 knobs. The Royal 780 sold for $99.95.

The "Golden Triangle" Royal 950 was carried through this model year with a slight variation in design. At first glance it looks identical to the previous year's model, but upon closer examination the second series set has a stepped design on the outer edge of the gray acrylic top. In addition, the "Wave-Magnet" antenna was relocated from the chassis and attached to the inside of the cabinet top.

Zenith dealers' ad showing "Golden Triangle" with its unique box.

CLOSED VIEW
OF DISPLAY CARTON

This beautiful, high quality inner display carton will add even more distinction, focus more consumer attention on the Zenith Golden Triangle . . . The World's Most Elegant Clock Radio. Every Golden Triangle is packaged in this stunning black velure covered display carton. Carton trimmed in gold color. Copy printed in gold and white. Base of carton acts as base for display purposes. Display carton with radio inside shipped in sturdy corrugated shipping carton.

Form No. 4-8243

PRINTED IN U.S.A.

A new entry to the line was a smaller pocket radio, the "Zenette," Royal 100. In response to the increasing pressure of Japanese imports, Zenith brought out this smaller, less costly radio in order to compete in the lower price field. This six transistor set, chassis 6ET42Z2, was still a fairly good performer, but the cabinet quality was inferior to most earlier models. Artificial metal trim soon wore off and the numbers on the dial scale quickly disappeared with use. This radio is hard to find in good condition. The Royal 100 was available in white, green, charcoal, yellow, or beige. The set retailed at $39.95 and was powered by three "AA" pen-lite batteries. Outstanding tone quality was produced by a 2-3/4 inch speaker, driven by an amplifier capable of up to 180 milliwatts of audio output.

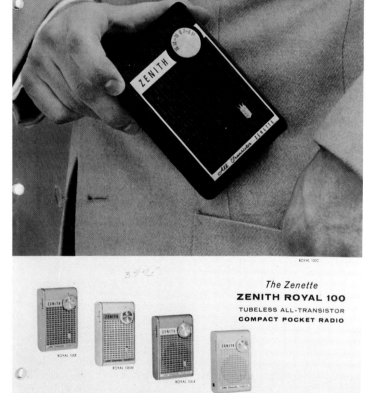

The Zenette
ZENITH ROYAL 100
TUBELESS ALL-TRANSISTOR
COMPACT POCKET RADIO

Zenith factory spec sheet photo, Royal 100.

34

Another all new model for this year was the first American-made all transistor cordless AM/FM portable radio, the "Trans-Symphony" Royal 2000. This eleven transistor set was incidentally the world's first portable with automatic frequency control for drift-free FM reception. This large portable, similar in size to the "Trans-Oceanic," was a real hot performer. The 11ET40Z2 chassis came equipped with tuned RF on both AM and FM, and was an exceptionally good receiver for long distance reception. The 5 x 7 inch speaker was driven by an amplifier capable of producing up to 500 milliwatts of undistorted audio output. Powered by a complement of eight "D" cells, the set has outstanding audio fidelity. Initially introduced at $189.95, the price was soon reduced to $149.95. This set is a fine example of Zenith quality, with its precision crafted hand-wired chassis. Two notable features available on this radio were a phono-jack which allowed one to play phonograph records through the radio and an adapter kit which allowed for use of this radio as an AM/FM tuner. The Royal 2000 is difficult to find in good condition.

Zenith factory spec sheet photo, Royal 2000.

Chapter 7

1960

The year 1960 brought further erosion of sales for American manufacturers of transistor radios. The Japanese were coming on strong with many new makes and models at very competitive prices. Zenith, unlike most other American companies who started buying their radios from offshore suppliers, continued to build their own sets in the United States. Zenith produced very few new models in 1960, however they made efforts to find new ways to be competitive in the lower price marketplace. Most of the recently redesigned 1959 models continued unchanged, however Zenith did introduce two new models for 1960.

The Royal 50 was introduced by Zenith as their shirt pocket sized competitor. The six transistor chassis, 6GT40Z1 or 6GT40Z2, was an exceptional performer for its size and would outperform nearly any shirt pocket sized imported set. The Zenith unit was powered by two inexpensive "AA" pen-lite cells which were readily available anywhere. It put out an amazing 135 milliwatts of audio output. The Royal 50 was available in several color combinations; these were white or black, or red, tan, or black with a white back. The Royal 50 sold for $29.95.

Another Zenith innovation was the Royal 55C, which was the convertible Royal 50 with a tabletop speaker case.

The Royal 50 could be placed into the cabinet, and it would then drive a large 4 inch speaker, giving it table radio performance. This set was available only in a charcoal colored cabinet and sold for $44.95. The Royal 55C "Converta" was truly a great all around performer, taking advantage of small size and room-filling performance. This set is quite rare to find complete and in good condition.

Zenith was still successful at designing and manufacturing radios using American parts and labor. Zenith's competitors, such as Motorola, General Electric, Sylvania, Magnavox, RCA, Admiral, Emerson, and Philco, were buying either complete radios, components, or both from Japanese suppliers. These companies would buy complete radios, with their respective names and logos on them, from the Japanese suppliers. It was a quick and easy way to put a product on the market without having to pay for the manufacturing plant or employees. All of these former American companies were soon taken over by foreign interests and only Zenith remained as an American owned company until the mid 1990s. In later years, however, even Zenith was forced to manufacture and purchase some products offshore.

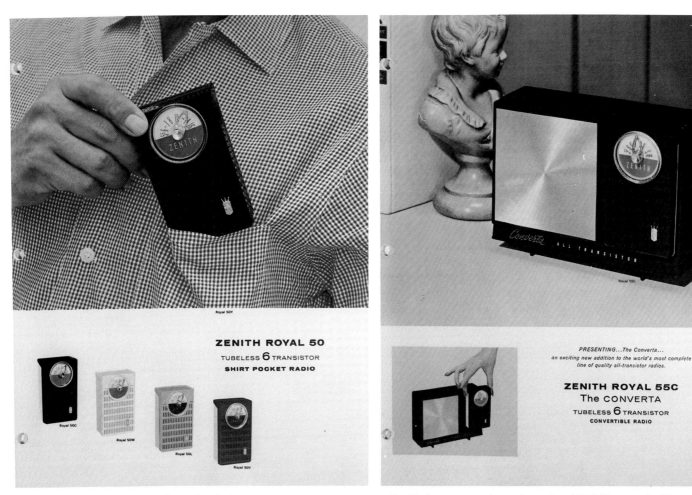

Zenith factory spec sheet photo, Royal 50.

Zenith factory spec sheet photo, Royal 55C "Converta" with special speaker box.

Zenith "Made in America" store dress-up kit.

Chapter 8

1961

In 1961 Zenith continued to introduce some of its most innovative and well made transistor radios. The Royal 50 enjoyed a successful year of production and was continued in 1961. The front of the cabinet was restyled to present a more modern appearance but the chassis was left unchanged. The cabinet was available in the same colors as the earlier Royal 50. In an effort to compete with the low priced radios from Japan, Zenith reduced the price of the Royal 50H to $19.95. The Royal 55 "Converta" was deleted from the line in 1961 due to poor sales numbers.

Zenith introduced two new shirt pocket models; the first, the Royal 90, featured modern styling for the '60s. This six transistor set, chassis 6JT40Z1, was still basically the same as the Royal 50 in performance and size. It came in four different color combinations, which were charcoal and white, beige and brown, orange and off-white, or all white, and was much different in appearance than the Royal 50. The Royal 90 was powered by two "AA" pen-lite batteries and retailed for $21.95.

Zenith factory spec sheet photo, Royal 50H.

Zenith factory spec sheet photo, Royal 90.

The other new offering was the Royal 125. This was also a six transistor set, chassis 6JT41Z2, and had the advantage of vernier tuning. It was otherwise very similar to the Royal 90. Available in three color combinations, yellow and white, beige and brown, or solid charcoal, this set sold for $24.95.

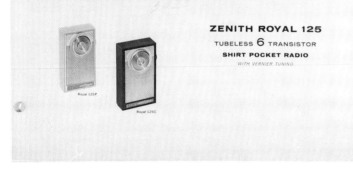

ZENITH ROYAL 125
TUBELESS 6 TRANSISTOR
SHIRT POCKET RADIO
WITH VERNIER TUNING

Zenith factory spec sheet photo Royal 125.

Another new addition to the 1961 Zenith line was the Royal 650. This six transistor set, chassis 6JT45Z1, was designed to fill the need for an inexpensive medium-sized portable set. With 350 milliwatts of audio output, it could easily fill a large area with sound. This radio was the product of cost-cutting measures, and the cabinet, even though quite stylish, was not to survive the ravages of time or the elements. It is very difficult to find one of these intact; the inexpensive "Permawear" cabinet material has usually crumbled and gone to pieces. The cabinet was available in three colors: ebony, ivory, or tan. Many other products made of this artificial leather type material suffered the same fate. Admiral Radio Corporation made many radios with this material and all came apart at the seams as well. Although the cabinet of the Royal 650 was deficient, the electronics were excellent and the overall performance was very good with adequate sensitivity and selectivity.

ZENITH ROYAL 650
TUBELESS 6 TRANSISTOR
PORTABLE RADIO

Zenith factory spec sheet photo, Royal 650.

Building on its leadership in black-and-white television, Zenith entered the color TV market in 1961, seven full years after RCA. But the new color TV emphasis at Zenith did not distract the company from continued leadership in transistor radios. For 1961, Zenith released an all new model to capture part of the lower priced market. This radio was the Royal 400. An all new "Extended Range" 3 x 5 inch speaker was used in this model. It was driven by an amplifier capable of 100 milliwatts of undistorted audio output. The audio response was still unusually good for such a small radio. Additional cost-cutting measures were used on the Royal 400. The seven transistor chassis 7GT40Z2 was powered by four "AA" pen-lite batteries. This set had no radio frequency amplifier stage. Zenith also used a much less complicated IF circuit and a plastic, rather than nylon, cabinet. This set sold for $39.95. The Royal 400 was still an above average performing radio and shared the same rich sound produced by the Royal 500H. The cabinet came in four different color combinations, which were ebony, white, two-toned brown, and two-toned green. Many Royal 400s have survived, but it is difficult to find one which is cosmetically intact. The very large metal speaker grilles were easily scratched or dented, and the metal badge carrying the Zenith name is frequently missing.

Zenith factory spec sheet photo, Royal 400.

Zenith factory spec sheet photo, Royal 475.

For 1961 the Royal 450 was redesigned and designated as the Zenith Royal 475. This seven transistor radio, chassis 7FT45Z1, was a powerful performer, putting out an amazing 450 milliwatts to drive a 3-1/2 inch Zenith quality speaker. It produced a rich beautiful tone quality. Although this set was a seven transistor design it still employed a tuned RF stage and vernier tuning which gave it very good sensitivity. Up to one hundred hours of listening pleasure could be enjoyed with six "AA" pen-lite batteries. Modern new styling graced the plastic cabinet of the Royal 475, which was available in beige or ebony and sold for $49.95.

Chapter 9

REBIRTH OF A LEGEND

Zenith dealer ad featuring exceptional speaker Royal 500H.

Zenith factory spec sheet information featuring extended range speaker.

The Royal 500, which remained the flagship of the Zenith compact transistor radio line, was totally redesigned in 1961 and new technologies were incorporated into its design. The cabinet was restyled to accent the amazing new 3 x 5 inch "Extended Range" speaker, while the radio still kept the same overall size and concept as the preceding Royal 500s.

The all new Royal 500H performance was greatly improved over previous models. Even though the audio output was increased from 100 milliwatts to 350 milliwatts, the set was still powered by a complement of four "AA" pen-lite batteries. The Royal 500H used the newly designed 3 x 5 inch Zenith speaker. This speaker was the culmination of efforts from the audio engineering staff in Zenith's Hearing Aid Division. The design was truly revolutionary. The speaker was one of the first products to incorporate use of ceramic magnet technology, new then but used extensively today. One of the most unusual things about this speaker design is the off-center voice coil. This technological breakthrough created a speaker with unusually wide frequency response and no resonant point, producing an extremely clear and transparent sound which had not been possible in a small radio before this time.

The totally new cabinet design of the Royal 500H gave the radio a modern look for the '60s. Many hours of research and development were spent in designing the acoustic chamber which was to house the 3 x 5 inch "Extended Range" speaker, and it was a marvel of audio engineering. Not only was great care taken to design a resonance free speaker, but the cabinet/acoustic chamber created for the Royal 500H was resonance free as well. The nylon cabinet had a well-vented back which allowed the speaker free movement and helped to avoid the resonance created by a sealed enclosure. To accommodate the improved circuitry of the Royal 500H in a cabinet of nearly the same dimensions as earlier models, it was necessary for Zenith to redesign and miniaturize many of the components incorporated into the set. Intermediate frequency and radio frequency transformers and coils were reduced to less than one-third the size of earlier designs. The tuning capacitor was an all new miniaturized design with vernier reduction which permitted precision movement for accurate tuning. The on/off switch and volume control was also redesigned and greatly improved over earlier designs. In addition, the Royal 500H had greatly improved station selectivity as a result of new advanced intermediate frequency amplifier circuitry. The use of four IF circuits with Zenith's exclusive IF transformer design gave this set the ability to tune in stations at nearly every 10 Khz on the dial without interference from adjacent stations. Coupled with the broadband RF amplifier and an exceptional audio circuit, this eight transistor radio, chassis 8HT40Z2, has proven to be an *unbeatable* performer for a pocket sized radio. The Royal 500H will outperform most radios many times its size; despite the many years since its introduction, it is almost impossible to find any other radio with better performance on the standard AM broadcast band than this set.

The Royal 500H was available in three colors, which were ebony, white, or two-toned gray cabinets molded of genuine nylon and accented with a beautiful gold speaker grille and escutcheon. The stand/carrying handle assembly was restyled and made more attractive and stronger than the bale wire handle used on earlier Royal 500s. The control knobs were recessed in a protected area at the top of the cabinet, which made tuning much easier than on earlier designs. This also prevented accidental movement of these knobs when the radio was placed in a pocket or purse.

The Royal 500H was truly the best pocket-sized radio ever made by Zenith, and was the product of many years of great innovation and careful attention to quality. Unfortunately, the pressures of world economics prevented any further improvements in subsequent models of the Royal 500.

The Royal 500H retailed for the price of $59.95 at a time when many imported sets sold for $25.00 to $30.00. Even Zenith came to realize that the profit making days for transistor radios were coming to a close, unless the radio filled an exclusive niche in the market place.

ZENITH ROYAL 500H DELUXE TUBELESS 8 TRANSISTOR **POCKET RADIO**

The world's richest tone quality in the world's finest performing pocket radio

MODEL 500WH   MODEL 500GH

Zenith factory spec sheet photo, Royal 500H.

Chapter 10

1962

INTRODUCING...FM BROADCAST RECEPTION IN THE

ZENITH 12 TRANSISTOR **TRANS-OCEANIC**

STANDARD BAND AND SHORTWAVE PORTABLE RADIO

THE ALL NEW **ZENITH ROYAL 3000**

POWERED TO TUNE IN THE WORLD...PROVIDES GLORIOUS FM FINE MUSIC ENTERTAINMENT

Zenith factory spec sheet photo, Royal 3000 "Trans-Oceanic.".

1962 brought more changes at Zenith. The "Trans-Oceanic" was redesigned and designated as the new Royal 3000 "Trans-Oceanic." The addition of FM reception was the most obvious change from the earlier Royal 1000 or Royal 1000D designs. The cabinet design was similar, but the knob arrangement and speaker grille were restyled. In addition, the back was redesigned to allow for the addition of FM sub-tuner circuits.

In circuitry, there were major changes, including the newly redesigned intermediate frequency amplifier circuits, which gave the Royal 3000 outstanding station selectivity just as with the Royal 500H. The audio section was also improved, with the inclusion of a new 6 x 4 inch speaker. The new Royal 3000 "Trans-Oceanic" was available with some exciting accessories, such as a Beat Frequency Oscillator (BFO) kit that allowed reception of sideband stations. There was also a genuine leather carrying case available as an optional accessory. Another rare accessory was the genuine Zenith "Trans-Oceanic" headphone set, which is seldom found. Zenith also produced an external antenna balum kit, which allowed the use of a long-wire antenna for not only the "Trans-Oceanic" but also many other Zenith transistor radio models. A detachable "Wave Magnet" antenna for use in shielded locations was also available as an optional accessory.

Chassis view showing BFO, top center switch and coil.

Zenith "Trans-Oceanic" head-phone set.

Zenith's careful attention to quality and the use of hand-wired construction on a metal chassis has resulted in the survival of many Royal 3000 sets. The chassis 12KT40Z3 contains a complement of twelve transistors and three germanium diodes plus an AFC diode. The FM tuner section which was added to the Royal 3000 is tuned by use of a three gang permeability tuning arrangement. This is accomplished by moving ferrous slugs through the cores of the tuning coils. In 1962 the Royal 3000 sold for $275.00, the Zenith Royal 1000 sold for $199.95, and the Royal 1000D "Trans-Oceanic" sold for $229.95.

For 1962 the Royal 50 was again restyled and improved. The six transistor chassis 6KT40Z1 was basically unchanged, but the cabinet was greatly improved. The tuning knob was recessed, and the radio could thus be placed in a shirt pocket without affecting the tuning. Earlier models had constantly been knocked off their dial settings when placed in a pocket because of the large exposed tuning knob. The performance of the Royal 50L was still outstanding for a shirt pocket radio. At the price of $19.95, this radio was truly an exceptional value. The Royal 50L was available in four different color combinations, which were charcoal, turquoise, yellow, or red, each accented with an off-white color cabinet front.

ZENITH ROYAL 50L
6 TRANSISTOR
SHIRT POCKET RADIO

Zenith factory spec sheet photo, Royal 50L.

The next step up from the Royal 50L was the all new Zenith Royal 130. Again, this set was similar in circuitry to the Royal 50, but had the advantage of vernier tuning and a slide rule dial. The six transistor radio, chassis 6KT 47Z1, was an exceptionally good performer. This stylish radio came in three colors: green, tan with a white front, or black with a white back. The Royal 130 was viewed as a bargain at $21.95.

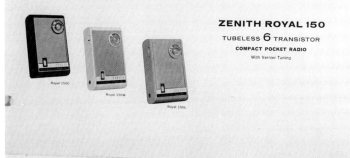

Zenith factory spec sheet photo, Royal 130.

The "Zennette" Royal 100 was upgraded in 1962 and designated as the Royal 150. This radio shared the same cabinet dimensions and chassis design as its predecessor but included the advantage of vernier tuning and nicer styling. The Royal 150 was offered in four different colors, which were charcoal, white, beige, or green, and it sold for $34.95.

Zenith factory spec sheet photo, Royal 150.

The Royal 400, Royal 475, Royal 500H, Royal 710LG, Royal 780YG, Royal 1000D, and Royal 2000 continued unchanged through the 1962 line, however, the Royal 500H has slight variations in the texture of the speaker grille, depending on which production run it came from.

Next in the line-up was the Royal 265. This radio shared the same features as the Royal 250, with the addition of vernier tuning. It was available in brown, ebony, or light beige and sold for $29.95.

ROYAL 265J

A new addition to the Zenith line was the "Super-Navigator" Royal 790Y. This three band radio, although very similar to the Royal 780, included a 2 - 4.9 Mhz Marine weather-navigation band. Like the earlier Royal 755, Zenith installed the antenna on the inside of the plastic handle. With the exception of this engineering oversight, the Royal 790Y "Super-Navigator" is an exceptionally well designed radio. This radio retailed at $99.95.

ZENITH ROYAL 265
TUBELESS 6 TRANSISTOR
POCKET RADIO

WITH VERNIER TUNING

Zenith factory spec sheet photo, Royal 265.

1962 was the last year that Zenith produced the Royal 675. The cabinet was restyled and a large, easier to operate tuning knob was employed. The fresh modern styling of this radio gave it an entirely different appearance. The circuitry was improved and the performance was exceptional. The Royal 675LG sold for $39.95.

The Royal 710LG continued basically unchanged, with the exception of its cabinet color. This set was now adorned in a brown charcoal "Permawear" cabinet accented with a chromium-plated speaker grille.

ZENITH ROYAL 675LG
TUBELESS 6 TRANSISTOR
PORTABLE RADIO

WITH VERNIER TUNING

Zenith factory spec sheet photo, Royal 675LG.

ZENITH ROYAL 710LG
TUBELESS 7 TRANSISTOR
PORTABLE RADIO

WITH VERNIER TUNING

Zenith factory spec sheet photo Royal 710LG.

ZENITH *Royal 790Y*

the SUPER-NAVIGATOR

SUPER-SENSITIVE · THREE-BAND
TUBELESS · 8 TRANSISTOR

PORTABLE RADIO

Super-sensitive receiver tunes the standard broadcast band, FAA weather-navigation stations on the 150 to 400 kc band and Marine weather-navigation and CAP stations on the 2 to 4.9 mc marine band . . . ideal for fliers, sailors, yachtsmen, tourists, outdoorsmen . . . and all who need outstanding reception of up to the hour weather reports, as well as long range reception of favorite programs on standard stations at home, in Europe or in the Tropics . . . on the beach . . . or while traveling.

**SELF-POWERED EMERGENCY NAVIGATIONAL AID
FOR PLANES AND BOATS**

Zenith factory spec sheet photo, Royal 790Y "Super-Navigator."

Chapter 11
1963

1963 was a year for major changes in the manufacturing process at Zenith. The economic problems created by low priced foreign competition forced Zenith to adopt less expensive methods of production. Lower cost materials were used to make many of the new models. Costly features, such as plug-in transistors and nylon cabinets, were deleted in the new model designs. Circuit changes were also made to reduce the cost of building these new models. Many new designs utilized an audio output circuit which contained no audio output transformer. The IF circuitry was far less sophisticated and contained fewer components. Top of the line sets such as the "Trans-Oceanic" and "Super-Navigator" models were still made with all of the deluxe features.

The Royal 50 was sold with two different cabinet designs. In an effort to use the remaining stock of old style Royal 50 cabinets, Zenith built the Royal 50K; at the same time, they also marketed the newly designed Royal 50L. Both of these sets sold for $19.95 and contained identical chassis.

Zenith introduced the all new shirt pocket Royal 60 in 1963; it contained a six transistor chassis, 6KT44Z1, nearly identical in design to the one used in the Royal 50. Modern styling, similar to that of the Royal 90, made this set quite attractive. The plastic cabinet was available in white, tan, or black. The Royal 60 sold for $21.95.

Zenith continued to produce the Royal 400 and the Royal 500H with no changes in circuitry or cabinetry.

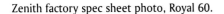

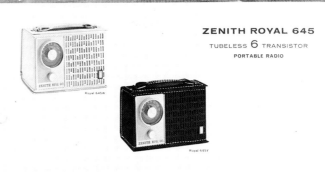

Zenith factory spec sheet photo, Royal 60.

Zenith factory spec sheet photo, Royal 645.

The Royal 645 was a new model for 1963. It replaced the Royal 650 and shared nearly identical features. This six transistor set, chassis 6KT45Z1, was exactly the same in performance as the Royal 650; the only difference between these radios was cabinet styling. This set was offered in three colors, which were ebony, a brown and beige two-tone, or an oyster white and brown two-tone. It retailed for $34.95.

Another new model was the Royal 670L, which replaced the Royal 675 and shared identical features and performance. This radio contained chassis 6KT41Z1, was available in a light brown "Permawear" cabinet accented with a gold color nickel-plated speaker grille, and could be purchased for $39.95.

The Royal 710LK, Royal 755LK, and the Royal 790YK were unchanged from earlier models with the exception of one feature, the "Battery Saver Circuit." Zenith intro-

duced this feature on these radios because other competing manufacturers had introduced similar circuitry on their models.

An all new concept for Zenith was their "Compact" AM/FM portable, the Royal 880 "Vocalaire." This nine transistor radio, chassis 9KT40Z6, was Zenith's first small portable AM/FM transistor radio. This radio had all the deluxe features offered by Zenith, such as a hand-wired chassis, plug-in transistors, tuned RF on both AM and FM, and advanced IF circuitry. The set put out 450 milliwatts into a 4 inch Zenith quality speaker. It operated on six "C" size batteries and sold for $89.95. The Royal 880 was available in a "Permawear" cabinet of either tan or ebony color, accented with nickel-plated trim.

Zenith continued models Royal 1000, Royal 1000D, Royal 2000, and Royal 3000 unchanged.

ZENITH ROYAL 670L
TUBELESS 6 TRANSISTOR
PORTABLE RADIO

Zenith factory spec sheet photo, Royal 670L.

ZENITH FM/AM PORTABLE TRANSISTOR RADIO
The Vocalaire Model ROYAL 880
The World's Finest Performing Personal Size FM/AM Transistor Radio

Zenith factory spec sheet photo, Royal 880.

Chapter 12
1964

1964 was the year that Zenith discovered difficulty in selling transistor radios. Some new models were introduced, some old models were continued, and some very innovative marketing strategies were employed by Zenith.

A new entry for 1964 was the Royal 40-G. This six transistor radio, chassis 6KT50Z1, was identical to the Royal 50. The biggest change in this radio was the cheaper cabinet with its artificial chrome trim. It came in three colors, brown, turquoise, or white, and sold for $18.95.

The Royal 50L and Royal 130 became the Royal 50L-G and Royal 130-G. These radios were unchanged from earlier models.

A new entry was the Royal 285-G. This eight transistor radio, chassis 8KT40Z2, was an effort by Zenith to continue the Royal 500 concept at a greatly reduced price. Even though this radio lacked the deluxe features of the Royal 500, its overall performance was still very good. It shared an identical chassis to the Royal 500E-1, which we will discuss later in this chapter. The Royal 285-G was available in a "Polystyrene" cabinet in four color combinations: green and white, brown and white, white and tan, or ebony. The set, compete with deluxe carry case, ear phone attachment, and batteries in a gift box, retailed for $34.95.

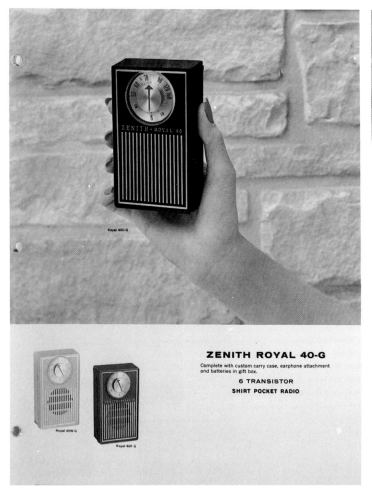

Zenith factory spec sheet photo, Royal 40-G.

Zenith factory spec sheet photo, Royal 285-G.

Early in 1964 the last of the Royal 500H radios was marketed. There were no changes in this set and it still sold for $59.95.

For the first half of the year, the Royal 645 remained unchanged. However, the radio was completely redesigned in both circuitry and cabinet appearance later in the year. The new Royal 645L was still a six transistor radio, chassis 6LT45Z2, but its performance was improved. A larger 4 inch speaker was employed and was still driven by an amplifier capable of up to 300 milliwatts output. With its elegant new fashion styling, this "Permawear" cabinet was available in ebony or beige, each accented by nickel-plated trim. This radio could be purchased from Zenith dealers for $34.95.

ZENITH ROYAL 645L
TUBELESS 6 TRANSISTOR
PORTABLE RADIO

Zenith factory spec sheet photo, Royal 645L.

By 1964 the price of transistor radios had begun a quick spiral downward. The Japanese were flooding the market with small radios for under $20.00, in some cases even less. Transistors became so inexpensive to produce that many manufactures did not care how many they used. It was becoming common to see ten, twelve, or fourteen transistor shirt pocket AM radios. In many circuits, only five or six transistors were actually useful in the radio circuitry; the rest were there as a marketing tool to better sell the radio. The general public was mostly unaware of this deceptive marketing technique. When good circuitry is used, a higher transistor count is usually an indicator of better performance, based on extra stages of RF, IF, or audio amplifier circuitry.

Due to the flood of inexpensive foreign sets, Zenith did not achieve expected sales numbers on many of its better models. As a result, the company found itself with a glut of leftover Royal 500E and Royal 500H cabinets, speakers, and chassis components. It was not possible to continue to build these great radios, sell them for greatly reduced prices, and still make a profit. The marketing and engineering staff at Zenith did, however, come up with a solution to the problem.

This solution lay in the 1964 release of two new models, the Royal 500E-1 and the Royal 500H-1. These radios look identical to their predecessors, yet there were big changes made in the electronics and physical layout of the new chassis. The Royal 500E-1 was still an eight transistor set, chassis 8KT40Z2. This was the newly designed, less expensive to manufacture chassis, also utilized in the Royal 285. The transistors were no longer the plug-in type. Zenith expanded the use of integrated networks which incorporated multiple components into one package. The audio output transformer was deleted from the circuit, and the speaker was direct coupled. This radio was still a good performer and was housed in the identical nylon cabinet used for the Royal 500E, allowing Zenith to reduce the oversupply of these leftover cabinets. The Royal 500E-1 sold for $39.95. The only way to determine the difference between a Royal 500E or a Royal 500E-1 is to remove the back and look inside.

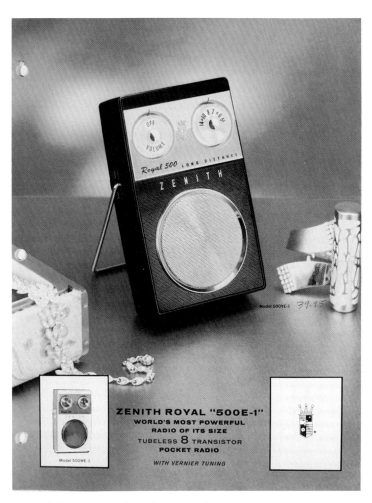

Zenith factory spec sheet photo, Royal 500E-1.

With the slow pace of sales for the Royal 500H, there was also an oversupply of cabinet and chassis components. Zenith redesigned the chassis and again reduced cost by eliminating the more expensive components. The eight transistor chassis, 8LT40Z1, was built with a less sophisticated IF circuit and the audio output transformer was again deleted from this circuit. The Royal 500H-1 was still an excellent radio with outstanding performance. The cabinet employed was identical to the earlier model, and at $39.95 the Royal 500H-1 was a real bargain. Both the Royal 500E-1 and the Royal 500H-1 helped Zenith to remain competitive at a time when prices were falling. These were the last of the really good Royal 500 radios.

At the same time, Zenith had released their all new Royal 500L. This radio, while quite modern and attractive, was a real step backwards in engineering for Zenith. The performance of the eight transistor chassis, 8LT45Z1, was reduced to only a shadow of its counterpart. The audio output fell to only 100 milliwatts, and the speaker size was reduced to 2-3/4 inches. The set sounded terrible with this inferior speaker and sealed enclosure cabinet. The tuning was more difficult and the ability to receive distant stations, when compared to earlier models, was poor. Zenith used more of the surplus parts, such as the Royal 500E battery compartment, the Royal 500H tuning capacitor, and the Royal 500H cabinet handle. The "Cycolac" cabinet was available in three colors: black, light green, or white. The black cabinet was complemented by a gold-tone front, while the white and light green models were equipped with a chrome panel. The Royal 500L came with a slide rule dial and was actually a very attractive radio. It was still powered by four "AA" pen-lite cells and sold for $39.95.

The Royal 500E chassis is pictured on the left and the Royal 500E-1 chassis is pictured on the right.

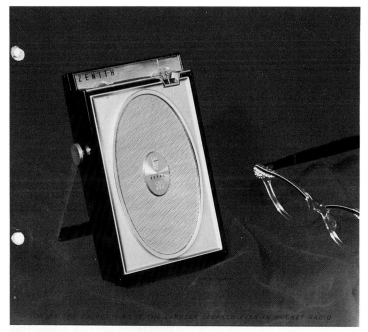

ZENITH ROYAL 500H-1 DELUXE TUBELESS 8 TRANSISTOR POCKET RADIO

The world's richest
tone quality in the
world's finest performing
pocket radio

MODEL 500WH-1   MODEL 500H-1

Zenith factory spec sheet photo, Royal 500H-1.

Model 500YL-G

39.95

ZENITH ROYAL 500L-G

Complete with deluxe carry case, earphone attachment
and batteries in gift box.

WORLD'S FINEST PERFORMING
POCKET RADIO

TUBELESS 8 TRANSISTOR
POCKET RADIO

WITH VERNIER TUNING

Model 500WL-G   Model 500FL-G

Zenith factory spec sheet photo, Royal 500L-G. (Note: Royal 500L photo not available, but set is identical in appearance.)

The Royal 500H chassis is pictured on the left and the Royal 500H-1 chassis is pictured on the right.

With this line-up, it was possible to purchase four different Royal 500 models in the same year for the same price of $39.95, with the exception of the remaining Royal 500H sets, which sold for $59.95 in early 1964.

The Royal 820 "Symphony" model, an all new, more compact AM/FM portable, was added to the line in 1964, replacing the Royal 880. This set was similar in circuitry and performance to the Royal 880, but its cabinet style and ease of use were greatly improved. The nine transistor chassis, 9LT42Z8, was a hand-crafted unit with all of Zenith's quality features. It produced excellent tone and volume, putting up to 450 milliwatts of audio into a 4 inch speaker. The Royal 820 was equipped with tuned RF on both AM and FM and could bring in distant reception very well. A complement of six "C" size batteries was used to power the set. The chrome and "Permawear" cabinet came in either charcoal or beige and the set was sold for $69.95.

The other models carried over from the 1963 lineup remained unchanged.

ZENITH FM/AM PORTABLE TRANSISTOR RADIO
The Symphony Model ROYAL 820

The World's Finest Performing FM/AM Transistor Radio

Zenith factory spec sheet photo, Royal 820.

Chapter 13

1965

1965 brought with it many changes, with respect to new models as well as new manufacturing processes. Cost cutting changes in both circuitry and parts sources were evident on most new models. Japanese components were used extensively on newly designed sets and cabinet quality was reduced.

New to the line was the Royal 80-G. This set used a totally new design and employed all of the cost saving changes that were needed to stay competitive, such as Japanese made components and the extensive use of integrated networks. This set, and many which followed it, were built with these changes. However, the performance remained above average because the Zenith engineering staff still designed the circuits. This eight transistor chassis, 8MT51Z8, was still powered by two "AA" pen-lite cells

and had an output of 100 milliwatts. The radio sold for $17.95, which was very competitive with foreign-made sets. The Royal 80-G was available in four color combinations: white with red, beige with white, white with green, or an all black model.

Zenith replaced the Royal 130 with the Royal 180-G. This radio was very similar in appearance, but had better circuitry than the Royal 130. The eight transistor chassis, 8MT50Z8, put out an amazing 200 milliwatts of audio and was powered by two "AA" pen-lite cells. Although Zenith used many foreign-made components in this set, its performance was still very good when compared with competing sets. The Royal 180-G was available in three color combinations, rust and white, ebony and white, or white and beige, and sold for $22.95.

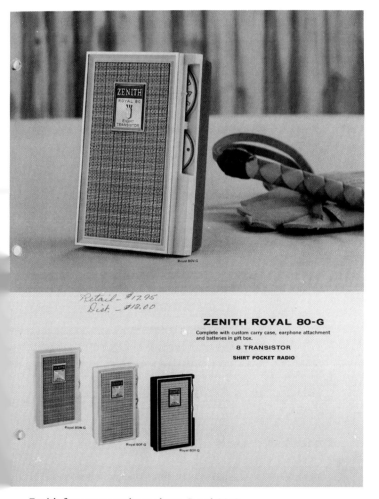

Zenith factory spec sheet photo, Royal 80-G.

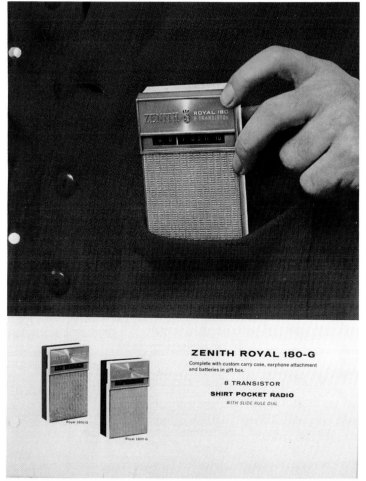

Zenith factory spec sheet photo, Royal 180-G.

Another change in the 1965 line-up was the release of the Royal 280G. This eight transistor set, chassis 8MT40Z2, was a direct replacement for the Royal 285. The chassis remained unchanged except for its number designation, and all performance characteristics were identical. The cabinet was styled more simply and was otherwise very similar to the Royal 285. Sold for $24.95, this radio gave Zenith the opportunity to compete in the low price field and still produce a high performance radio.

Zenith factory spec sheet photo, Royal 280-G.

The Royal 500L was modified and released as the Royal 500L-G. This set may be found with the original eight transistor chassis, 8LT45Z1 or 8LT45Z3, but later production sets contained chassis 8MT45Z8. Sets containing this latter chassis were the first Royal 500s to be built with foreign-made components. The IF transformers, audio driver transformer, and electrolytic capacitors were all Japanese-made. The circuitry was basically the same as used on the earlier chassis. This set was a poor example to carry the Royal 500 name. Retailing at $39.95, not very many of these were sold. The price was still too high to compete with foreign sets and there was nothing special about the performance of this radio. The colors were the same as those available on the Royal 500L.

Zenith factory spec sheet photo, Royal 500L-G.

Late 1965 brought with it the final step in the "Evolution Of A Classic." This radio, the Royal 500N-G, was totally redesigned and no longer followed the Royal 500 concept. The new set was a horizontally oriented, compact portable with poor performance and even worse styling. The eight transistor chassis, 8NT40Z8 or 8NT40Z9, had an output of only 100 milliwatts and the inexpensive 2-3/4 inch speaker had terrible sound reproduction. Tuning this radio was difficult with the drive system used. Four "AA" pen-lite cells were used to power the Royal 500N-G and Zenith again used more of the old Royal 500E battery compartments. The plastic cabinet was a sealed enclosure, which added to the poor sound produced by the radio. It was available in white or charcoal, each accented by a chrome-plated speaker grille and dial scale. The handle employed was too small and was also too loosely mounted on the cabinet. It is unfortunate that the last in such a great line of radios would be represented by this final, cheaply designed and fabricated radio.

Zenith factory spec sheet photo, Royal 500N-G.

Zenith factory spec sheet photo, Royal 555-G "Sun-Charger."

Although it was no longer economically prudent for Zenith to invest in transistor radio research and development during the mid '60s, one imaginative design was employed in conjunction with the last Royal 500. This unique design utilized a solar battery array, which was housed in the handle of the new "Sun Charger" Royal 555-G. Other companies had produced solar powered transistor radios before Zenith, but none did it as well as Zenith. The radio came equipped with rechargeable batteries and was also equipped with a built-in 110 volt A.C. power supply which could be used to either charge the batteries or operate the radio. This radio shares an identical chassis with the Royal 500N-G, except for the addition of the solar array and power supply. The Royal 555-G "Sun Charger" was available in two colors, charcoal and white, and sold for $59.95.

The Royal 645 continued unchanged from the previous year.

Another new entry in the transistor line was the Royal 705. This set was smaller, lighter, and much less well-constructed than the Royal 700 series radios which preceded it. Zenith was still attempting to reduce their supply of surplus parts from earlier designs and the Royal 705 was full of these parts. A Royal 500 battery compartment, Royal 450 tuning capacitor, Royal 500E-1 volume control, and many Japanese components were utilized in the seven transistor chassis, 7MT45Z8. This set still delivered better than average performance, but certainly would not compete with earlier Zenith models. The Royal 705 was powered by four "AA" pen-lite batteries and did deliver up to 200 milliwatts to its 3-1/2 inch speaker. The "Permawear" cabinet came in two colors, ebony or brown, each accented with a chrome die cast front and a black and silver speaker grille. The Royal 705 sold for $29.95.

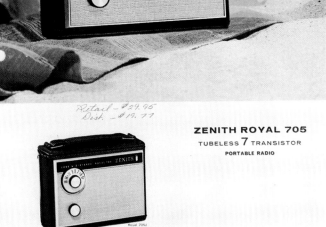

Retail — $29.95
Dist. — $19.77

ZENITH ROYAL 705
TUBELESS **7** TRANSISTOR
PORTABLE RADIO

ZENITH ROYAL 710M
7 TRANSISTOR
PORTABLE RADIO

Featuring • New Tone Control Switch
• Provision For External AC Power Supply

Zenith factory spec sheet photo, Royal 705.

Zenith factory spec sheet photo, Royal 710M.

The Royal 710M was the last of the Royal 710 line. The cabinet was restyled and featured a slide rule dial. The quality of this cabinet was considerably lower than on earlier models. The seven transistor chassis, 7MT43Z2, was an all new design and incorporated many of the new cost-cutting features. The performance of this set was not very good when compared with earlier Royal 710 sets. This radio used a complement of six "C" cell batteries, and audio output was still good at 500 milliwatts. Selling for $34.95, the Royal 710M came in either ebony or olive.

The Royal 755 also made its last appearance in 1965, employing a completely redesigned cabinet and chassis. The styling for this radio and the new Royal 790YM "Super-Navigator" were very similar and both featured a larger, easier to use tuning knob. The eight transistor chassis, 8MT41Z2, had an output of 500 milliwatts and was driven into a 4 inch speaker. The sound of this radio was exceptionally good, but sensitivity and selectivity were not as good as earlier Royal 755 models and long distance reception was more difficult. The Royal 755M was still powered by six "C" cell batteries. One major improvement was the relocation of the ear phone jack to the left side of the cabinet. This finally overcame the annoying problem of having to open the cabinet in order to access the jack. The Royal 755M was housed in a cabinet of genuine leather, either beige or black, with a chromium-plated grille. It retailed for $49.95.

The Royal 790YK or 790YM "Super-Navigator" underwent a major change, with styling similar to the Royal 755M. The eight transistor chassis, 8MT43Z3, was an all new design, and *no* short cuts were used in its design. All of Zenith's quality features were employed, and even further improved circuitry was used. This was the best of the "Super-Navigator" radios and Zenith continued this design until the last of these radios were produced.

Zenith factory spec sheet photo, Royal 755M.

Zenith factory spec sheet photo, Royal 790YM "Super-Navigator."

The 790YM was a three-band receiver which covered the 150-400 Khz FAA Weather Navigation and European Long Wave Broadcast band, the 550-1600 Khz Standard Broadcast band, and the 2-5 Mhz Marine-Navigation and Civil Air Patrol band. It was built with tuned RF on all bands and came equipped with a direction finding (DF) level control. In normal position the set has automatic gain control, but in the DF level position adjustable manual gain control allows for build and fade orientation and cone identification for aviators. A rotating housing which contained the three antennas used on this set allowed for easy direction finding. The set also came equipped with a tuning meter, which helped with direction finding as well as accurately tuning stations. The large slide rule dial came with a pilot light, which illuminated the dial tuning meter, and a top mounted azimuth for quick night readings. The heavy duty 4 inch speaker was driven by an amplifier capable of up to 500 milliwatts output. A new tone control allowed for selection of the desired tone. The Royal 790YM had provisions for either miniature or 1/4 inch head phone plugs. Six "C" cell batteries provided up to three hundred hours of service on one set.

Zenith offered a Beat Frequency Oscillator Kit as an accessory, which allowed for reception of amateur code and single side-band signals. The cabinet of the Royal 790M was constructed with genuine top grain black cowhide accented with a metal grille and attractive top carry handle. Selling for $109.95, the Royal 790M was truly a bargain. Although many Zenith models suffered from the economics of the mid '60s, the "Super-Navigator" and "Trans-Oceanic" models continued to be improved and their design and construction remained of high quality.

Chapter 14
INNOVATIVE ENGINEERING AT ZENITH

NEWS from

Zenith Radio Corporation
6001 W. Dickens Avenue
Chicago 39, Illinois

FOR IMMEDIATE RELEASE

9-2-54

A tiny, new all-transistor hearing aid, the Royal-M, is being added to Zenith Radio Corporation's export line, it was announced today by John A. Miguel, Jr., manager of Zenith's international division.

He said that the Royal-M is slightly larger and about the same weight as a Zippo cigarette lighter. The instrument is completely tubeless, has a full complement of three junction-type transistors, and is as powerful as some hearing aids at least twice its size and as many selling for twice its price or more.

Miguel pointed out that the Royal-M operates on a single inexpensive dry-cell battery that is available through any Zenith dealer. It needs no bulky "B" battery.

Shipment of the Royal-M is now being made to many Zenith export distributors, Miguel said. The first of Zenith's revolutionary new 3-transistor hearing aids, the Royal-T*, was made available to the export market in May of this year, he stated.

"Testing in the United States," Miguel said, "shows that the Royal-M provides a week of normal full-day service, with a battery cost of about forty cents a month as compared to $4.50 to $9.00 per month for vacuum tube aids of comparable power."

Equipped with a new Permaphone microphone, the Royal-M offers improved clarity over its entire tone and volume range. It is resistant to high temperature and humidity, a feature of great importance in trouble-free life for a hearing aid.

*Reg. U.S. Pat. Off.   MORE...

As in all other Zenith hearing aids, the controls are located outside the case for easy fingertip adjustment by the wearer. The volume control gives smooth, continuous increase in power from the lowest to the highest volume. An improvement has been made in the four-position tone control to provide greater differential and clarity in its various positions. This feature enables the wearer to adjust the tone to varying conditions throughout the day.

The Royal-M is equipped with an ingenious, simple carrying clip. It also includes the traditional Zenith feature of low clothing noise and is covered by the Zenith warranty and service plan which provides for low-cost maintenance through the years,

- 30 -

Official Zenith press release, September 2, 1954.

The long tradition of imaginative and innovative engineering at Zenith continued to flourish during the first ten years of the company's transistor product technology. Zenith was a pioneer in the application of transistor technology. The company's Hearing Aid Division began working with transistors in 1949, and produced the first transistorized hearing aid in 1952. This three transistor model Royal T was a major advance in the efficiency and performance of hearing aids; battery economy was increased by 96 percent over vacuum tube models. There were some problems with early production, but by October 1953 the units were released for general distribution. Zenith's share of the hearing aid market went up tremendously.

The field of acoustical performance was one of the more important areas the Zenith team worked to improve. One of the most common complaints that consumers had toward small transistor radios was that they sounded "tinny," that is, they lacked the ability to produce a full spectrum of sound. Some produced distorted sound, due to poor circuitry, very poor speaker design, or both. Many were plagued with speakers and cabinets which made them very unbalanced in frequency response. These sets usually had a very distinct resonant point which "colored" the sound and made for unpleasant listening. Zenith was quite aware of these problems.

In order to maintain the Zenith reputation for high performing and excellent sounding radios, the company worked hard to come up with solutions to these problems. The circuitry used on Zenith's early radios was very good and capable of producing excellent audio when coupled with a large speaker. The primary deficiency was in the speakers used for these early models. There was also some room for improvement in cabinet design, in order to keep the sound chamber from being resonant, and thus "coloring" the sound. Since the Hearing Aid Division engineers had done much research on audio response, they were the ones who worked on the improvements of these sets.

One major change appeared in the 1958 Zenith Royal 500D. The reverse cone speaker found in some of these sets gives the radio better sound projection as well as slightly increased audio fidelity.

Zenith reverse cone speaker from 1958.

This design was continued and may also be found in some 1960-61 Royal 500E sets. At the end of 1961 Zenith was to revolutionize the performance standards for compact transistor radios. The product selected to showcase the best of many newly designed advances was the Royal 500H transistor radio. Major advances in RF-IF and audio circuitry were incorporated in this set, but the most unusual and innovative feature contained in this radio was the 3 x 5 inch "Extended Range" speaker. The size of this speaker in such a small radio was unusual, yet even more unusual was the design of the speaker itself. Instead of placing the voice coil in the center of the speaker, Zenith engineers designed the "Extended Range" speaker with an off-center voice coil located about one-third of the way from one end of the speaker and two-thirds of the way from the other end. This arrangement created a speaker with no resonant point in its sound reproduction. Another major benefit of this design is a wide range frequency response, producing crisp-clear highs and delightfully rich low notes, with excellent sound on all frequencies in-between. This Zenith "Extended Range" speaker was also one of the first consumer electronic products to utilize the new—at that time—ceramic magnet structure technology. This design resulted in much greater speaker efficiency and compactness.

Nearly all speakers use this magnet technology today. The improved performance provided by the Zenith "Extended Range" speaker was further enhanced by the use of a newly designed cabinet for the Royal 500H. The primary focus of this cabinet design was to accommodate the "Extended Range" speaker and to enhance frequency response. An engineering staff in the Hearing Aid Division, led by Dwight Poppy and Donald Knight, was largely responsible for the acoustic research which resulted in the design of the Royal 500H speaker and sound-chamber cabinet.

Zenith also went the extra mile in its chassis designs. Most were designed to be very easily serviced. Features such as plug-in transistors made transistor replacement much easier than with soldered in units. Zenith was careful to make most components readily accessible on the chassis. The quality of components was exceptional and most have survived the years.

Zenith's use of a "hand-crafted" chassis was used extensively on the "Navigator" and "Trans-Oceanic" models. Some of the larger AM-FM portables such as the Royal 820, Royal 880, and Royal 2000 also featured the hand-crafted chassis, as did the first year Royal 500. This labor-intensive method of building radios was not maintained by any of the other radio manufactures after the late 1950s. Zenith, however, continued using it until the late 1970s, with the Royal D7000Y "Trans-Oceanic." The durability and performance of these radios is legendary.

Zenith extended range speaker, part #49U963, used in Royal 500H radio.

Chapter 15

CLONES

In the history of manufactured products, there have been many instances where a successful design was copied by other companies making a similar product. The experience of Zenith Radio Corporation was no exception, and If one looks at postwar radio designs it is possible to see many examples of this practice.

"Trans-Oceanic" Clones

With the great success of the Zenith "Trans-Oceanic" there soon followed many radios, by many different companies, which copied the "Trans-Oceanic" concept. With the release of the first transistorized "Trans-Oceanic" in 1957, it wasn't long before most competing manufacturers had their own models of similar design.

The Magnavox Company of Fort Wayne, Indiana introduced their "Inter-Continental" model AW100 for sale in 1957, around the same time as the first transistor "Trans-Oceanic." This multi-band short-wave radio is an excellent performer and is very well constructed. It is unfortunate that Magnavox did not continue production of this radio, as the AW100 was a worthy competitor to the "Trans-Oceanic."

Philco Radio Corporation released their "Trans-World" model T9 in 1958. This large multi-band portable was very well designed and constructed. It featured a large easy-to-read dial scale and very smooth flywheel tuning. The audio output and tone quality were exceptional. Short-wave reception with the T9 was particularly good. Extreme sensitivity and intelligibility made this one of the best radios for short-wave listening.

However, neither of these models was as cosmetically pleasing or as durable as the "Trans-Oceanic," and few good examples of either survive today.

Magnavox "Inter-Continental" model AW100 radio.

Philco "Trans-World" model T9 radio.

In 1958 the Admiral Corporation released their "All-World" model 909. This radio was well made and performed very well, but due to low sales numbers and difficult serviceability very few of these sets are found today. Admiral followed this set with their model 1009, which included FM reception in order to compete with the Zenith Royal 3000 "Trans-Oceanic."

In 1958, RCA introduced their "Strato-World" transistor portable, model 1-MBT-6. This multi-band set did not even begin to compete with the "Trans-Oceanic." The circuitry was poorly designed, crudely built, and difficult to service. The cabinet was cheaply constructed and made from inferior materials. Because few examples of this set survive today, it is a very collectible set for the transistor radio enthusiast.

General Electric released their "World Monitor" model P990 several years after the release of the "Trans-Oceanic." The "World Monitor" was a less than great performer and

Admiral "All-World" model 909 radio.

proved very difficult to service. This multi-band radio is not very aesthetically pleasing, and very few are found in good condition.

The Heath Company of Benton Harbor, Michigan, produced a model GR43, which was a multi-band radio kit, designed to be assembled by the owner. This model closely resembles the Zenith Royal 3000 "Trans-Oceanic;" the physical similarities between these two sets are remark-able. The rotary dial scale and control positions, for example, are identical. Although these sets look so similar, the circuitry and chassis layout are entirely different. None-theless, the GR43 had a limited production because Zenith required Heath to cease production due to patent infringement. Ironically, Zenith later owned Heath from 1979 through 1989.

RCA "Strato-World" model 1-MBT-6 radio.

General Electric "World Monitor" model P990 radio.

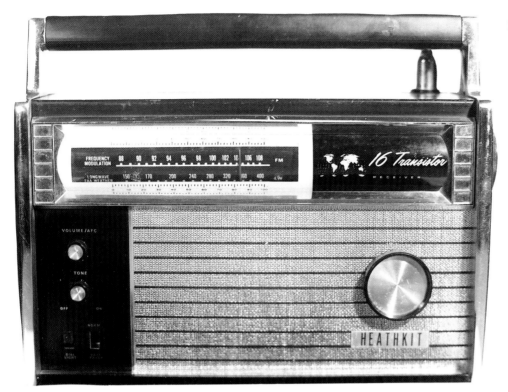

There were also "Trans-Oceanic" clones from foreign sources, including Realtone, JVC, Juliette, Philips, Lloyd's, and many others, but the one that seemed to most obviously copy the Zenith concept was the Sony "Earth Orbiter," models CRF 5090 and CRF 5100. Again the rotary dial scale and tuning knob configuration were extremely similar, however this time the Zenith Royal 7000 "Trans-Oceanic" was the set to be copied.

Royal 50 Clones

The Zenith Royal 50 shirt pocket portable was another very well-received radio, and it wasn't long before "look alike" models appeared. This time, a model designated as TS10 was marketed by music stores and large department store chains. Each store used its own trade name for this set. Names such as Jewel, Grinnels, Hudson, Ambassador, Majestic, and others were used. In styling, the TS10 is a

Sony "Earth Orbiter" model CRF 5090 radio.

hybridization of the Zenith Royal 50 and the RCA model 3RH21. The front design closely resembles the RCA but the rest of the cabinet design is a direct takeoff on the Royal 50 design.

As usual, the transistor count was higher than that of the original radio being copied. As noted earlier, this was done in order to mislead the buying public into thinking that there would be better performance. Unfortunately, the design of these sets was poor and performance did not compare with the real thing. Even though the TS10 contained ten transistors, only six were used in the circuit correctly—the other four were there only to make it a ten transistor radio! This practice was to become more common as the price of transistors fell. It is possible to find a twenty-one transistor, shirt pocket, AM only radio, which really uses only six of the transistors to advantage in a conventional super-heterodyne circuit.

Side view: clone on left, Zenith Royal 50 on right.

Zenith Royal 50 flanked by two Jewel clones.

Royal 50 clones: Grinnells on left, RCA in center, and Royal 50 on the right.

Royal 500 Clones

One of the most copied of all transistor radios was the famous Zenith Royal 500. Because this model set the performance standard by which most other radios were compared, it wasn't long before many variations on its design appeared. The variety of "Royal 500" concept radios ranges from sets which are almost identical copies to sets which copied only the basic Royal 500 concept. Since the Royal 500 was produced from 1955 until 1965, there were many variations which appeared throughout the Royal 500's evolution.

One of the closest copies appeared in England in 1958. Marketed as a "Webster," this set so closely resembles the Royal 500 that at first glance you would not see the difference. The cabinet styling and dimensions are identical, presumably molded as an exact copy of the Royal 500 cabinet, and the dial script is very similar.

Front view: Zenith on left and Webster on right.

Rear view: Zenith on left and Webster on right.

Side view: Zenith on left and Webster on right.

Although this Webster clone is a dead ringer for the Zenith in appearance, that is where the similarity ends. The chassis is of an entirely different design and is of inferior quality. The construction of the chassis is almost primitive and not very durable.

Front view: Gimbels on left and Zenith on right.

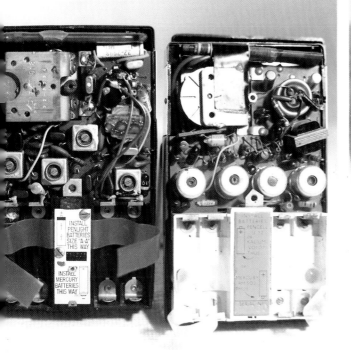

Chassis view: Zenith on left and Webster on right.

The Webster uses six transistors and is not a very powerful performer. Powered by four "AA" pen-lite cells, the battery compartment is nearly identical to the Zenith. Not many of these were produced, and they were never marketed in the United States.

The same marketing organization which distributed the Royal 50 clone, model TS10, also had Royal 500 clones. These sets were similarly marketed under house names and were produced with many variations. The exact Royal 500 cabinet dimensions and bale type handle were utilized. The battery holder and ear phone connector were located identically. Some earlier versions used knobs very similar to the Royal 500 and the script for dial indication and on/off/volume was an exact replica.

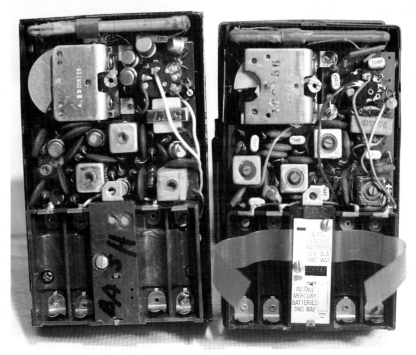

Chassis view: Gimbels on left and Zenith on right.

Zenith dial script

Gimbels dial script

Probably the most interesting thing about these sets was their complete copy of the Royal 500 chassis. Most components were placed identically to the Zenith's and small details such as the design of the back screw tab were duplicated. The clone chassis sometimes contained eight, sometimes ten, and sometimes twelve transistors. Only seven transistors were usefully employed in the circuitry. The chassis, which directly copied Zenith's, was produced in 1959, 1960, and 1961.

In 1962 the chassis and circuitry of the clones were totally redesigned, although the Royal 500 style cabinet concept continued in the later models. The names found on the Royal 500 type radios were Ambassador, Hudson, Gimbels, Grinnels, Artone, Jewel, Cosmopolitan, Majestic, and others. These sets were made in the USA and did contain some foreign components.

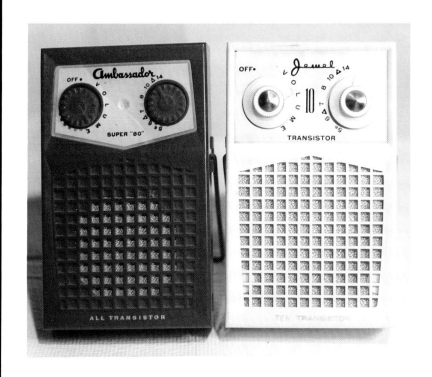

Other variations of Royal 500 clones.

Later cabinet style for Royal 500 clones.

Major American competitors also followed the Zenith design with their own sets. Most of these radios resembled the Zenith in size and concept, but were not direct copies. RCA made several sets which bore a resemblance, but which did not exhibit the high performance needed to compete with the Zenith sets. Motorola followed Zenith's lead in producing their model X16, which was also the same size and style. This Motorola was a fairly good performer, as were most Motorola radios.

Admiral Corporation had over the years produced many radios which looked as though they were inspired by Zenith designs. Admiral took a slightly different approach to the Royal 500 type radio. They turned it on its side for a horizontal style and used a similar size, as well as the familiar bale type adjustable handle. The battery compartment and chassis layout were very similar to the Zenith design.

Royal 500 style RCA on left and Motorola on right.

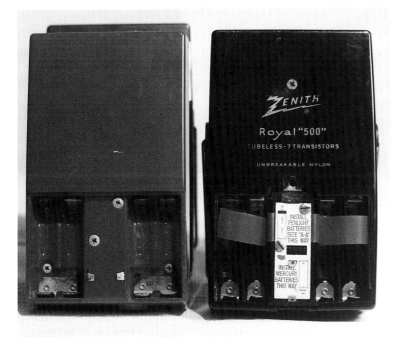

Zenith Royal 500 on right and Admiral model 801 pictured on left. The Admiral has been placed vertically to better illustrate its similarity to the Zenith.

Late model Admiral clones, similar to Zenith Royal 500L.

The Admiral models included a four transistor base, model 4P28, five transistor model 582, seven transistor model 7M12, and eight transistor model 801. The performance of these sets was consistent with the amount of circuitry each contained. The four and five transistor models were weak, but the seven transistor model worked quite well. The eight transistor set had vernier tuning and a broadband RF amplifier stage which gave it performance close to that of the Royal 500D and Royal 500E. The Admi-

ral model Y2421GP closely resembled the Royal 500L. Admiral also released model Y2531GP which was a ten transistor AM-FM model, styled similarly. Both of these latter models were made in Japan for Admiral.

Interestingly, even the clones were sometimes cloned, and the Admiral was one that was cloned by the Japanese. These Gloritone and Excel sets both share a striking resemblance to the early Admiral sets.

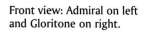
Front view: Admiral on left and Gloritone on right.

Rear view: Admiral on left and Gloritone on right.

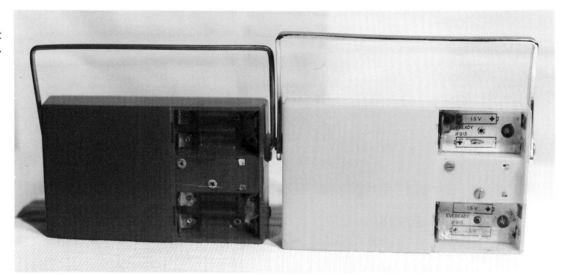

Excel on left and Admiral on right.

The Japanese sold this type of set under many names. However, the performance of the Japanese sets did not even approach that of the Zenith or the better Admiral sets.

In later years, Admiral sets retained the size and format of the company's earlier sets, but were restyled to reflect changing taste. Admiral continued to produce models having from five to eight transistors.

The practice of cloning the Royal 500 continued even after Zenith redesigned this set for the 1962 model year. The Royal 500H was soon followed to the marketplace by Lloyd's model TR800. This set was oriented horizontally instead of vertically, but appeared to be an obvious copy of the Zenith design.

This Japanese clone is nearly the same size as the Zenith and, like the Zenith, it employs eight transistors. The performance is quite good for a Japanese set, however it falls far short of the Zenith's. Behind the large oval speaker grille of the Lloyd's is a 3 inch round speaker, with the extra area filled by a cardboard spacer. Although the handle/stand assembly looks nearly identical to the Zenith's, it is made from thin metal which is very flimsy and easily bent.

Royal 500H on left and Lloyd's TR800 on right.

Side view: Zenith on left and Lloyd's on right.

The horizontal bar which accents the volume and tuning controls is plastic on the Lloyd's, unlike the cast metal unit on the Royal 500H. However, the styling looks almost identical, including the knob design.

The Lloyd's TR800 is one of the very few Japanese sets which used nylon for its cabinet material. In an effort to closely copy the Zenith, the Japanese made the choice to use this cabinet material. The script on the back is similar to that used on the Zenith and proclaims "Unbreakable Nylon" just like on the Zenith, however it also admits to being "Made in Japan." The venting in the back is also very similar to the Zenith, and even the screws and hardware associated with the back look amazingly like those used on the Royal 500H. The Lloyds radio retailed at $59.50, exactly 45 cents less than the Zenith.

Royal 500H dial script.

Lloyd's dial script.

Rear view: Zenith on left and Lloyd's on right.

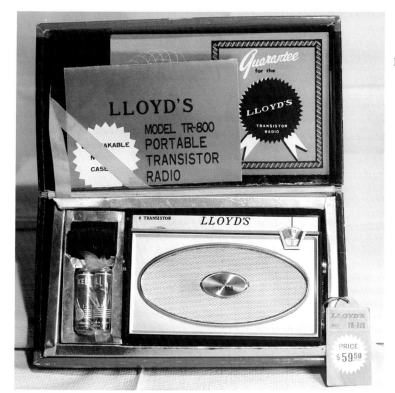

Lloyd's model TR800 in gift box.

Exterior view of Lloyd's model TR800 gift box.

These sets were sold for less than list price in discount and department stores and few of them are found today. Poor marketing and fierce competition from less expensive models caused extremely small sales numbers. There are other trade names used for this radio, as was frequently the case with imported sets. For the serious Zenith Royal 500 collector, this is a very prized set to add to the collection, as it was such a obvious effort to duplicate the Zenith product. The Lloyd's TR800 and the Webster are two of the best examples found which illustrate the cloning of the Zenith Royal 500.

The Bulova Watch Company had long been in the radio business and had sold many models of transistor radios. In 1958 they released their model 660. This radio was the same size and concept as the Royal 500 but looked much different, thanks to a different approach in styling. The chassis, however, is almost identical to the Royal 500's seven transistor chassis, 7ZT40. The component locations are the same and many parts look as though they came from the same supplier.

Front view: Bulova on left and Zenith on right.

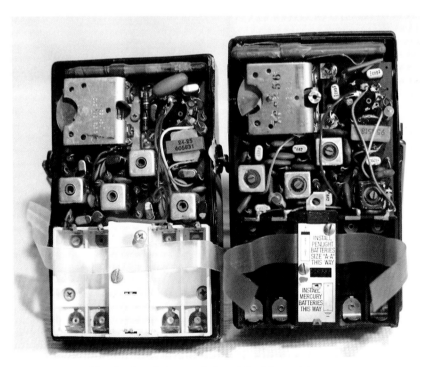

Chassis view: Bulova on left and Zenith on right.

In 1959 the Grundig Company of Germany also produced a Royal 500 type radio. This radio, model 1059, shared the size and styling of the Royal 500 and had some similar chassis characteristics. It is a good performer with excellent sound reproduction and good sensitivity.

Royal 675, 700, 750 Clones

The Royal 675, 700, and 750 type radios were also the subject of cloning. The Japanese soon released their leather-clad look-alikes in order to capture that part of the market. Most of these sets were poor performers and did not come close to the quality produced by Zenith. They were sold under many "American" sounding names, such as "GM Sportsman," "Americana," and others. There was also a "Super-Navigator" clone from Japan. This set was sold in airports, and from the outside it closely resembled

the Royal 780. Marketed as the "Weathercaster," model ST-8J, this set was very poorly made by comparison.

The Admiral Corporation followed Zenith's lead and produced their own "Super-Navigator" style radio. This eight transistor radio, model Y2137, was designated as the "Admiral Clipper" and shared the same physical dimensions and performance characteristics as the Zenith unit. The frequency coverage and navigational features were identical. This "hand-wired" unit from Admiral was a worthy competitor to Zenith and featured an unusually beautiful dial scale which made accurate tuning very easy. This set was also powered by a complement of six "C" sized cells and it performed very well. This set is difficult to find in good condition because of the inexpensive artificial leather cabinet used.

Front view: Grundig model 1059 on left and Zenith on right.

Back view: Grundig model 1059 on left and Zenith on right.

Zenith Royal 790 "Super-Navigator."

Weathercaster, model ST-8J.

Admiral "Clipper", model Y2137.

Chapter 16
MILITARY TRANSISTORIZED "TRANS-OCEANIC" MODELS

Three military transistorized Trans-Oceanic models have been identified. These sets are shown in Zenith records, but very little information is available.

The first model was the "R1000 (M)." This receiver was based on the Royal 1000 design with many modifications.

Zenith photo showing R1000 (M) transistorized military "Trans-Oceanic" type receiver.

The R1000 (M) had the addition of a front-mounted tuning meter, located just above the volume knob. The "Wave-Rod" antenna-handle was deleted and an external antenna connector was placed were it had been located. This Trans-Oceanic model also featured different frequency coverages than the civilian model. The early version of the R1000 (M) featured continuous coverage from 100 Khz up to 30 Mhz. In place of the tone control there was a BFO control which allowed for reception of code and single side-band signals.

The set was housed in a carrying case/backpack made of strong canvas, which also housed a small tape recorder. This tape recorder allowed recording of signals received by the R1000 (M).

A second version of the R1000 (M) featured extended frequency coverage. In addition to the standard coverage, a four section inductive tuner was installed, giving this receiver the capability of reaching from 20 to 80 Mhz in one band and from 75 to 205 Mhz in the next band. This Trans-Oceanic model was tailor-made for the Central In-

Zenith photo showing close-up of R1000 (M).

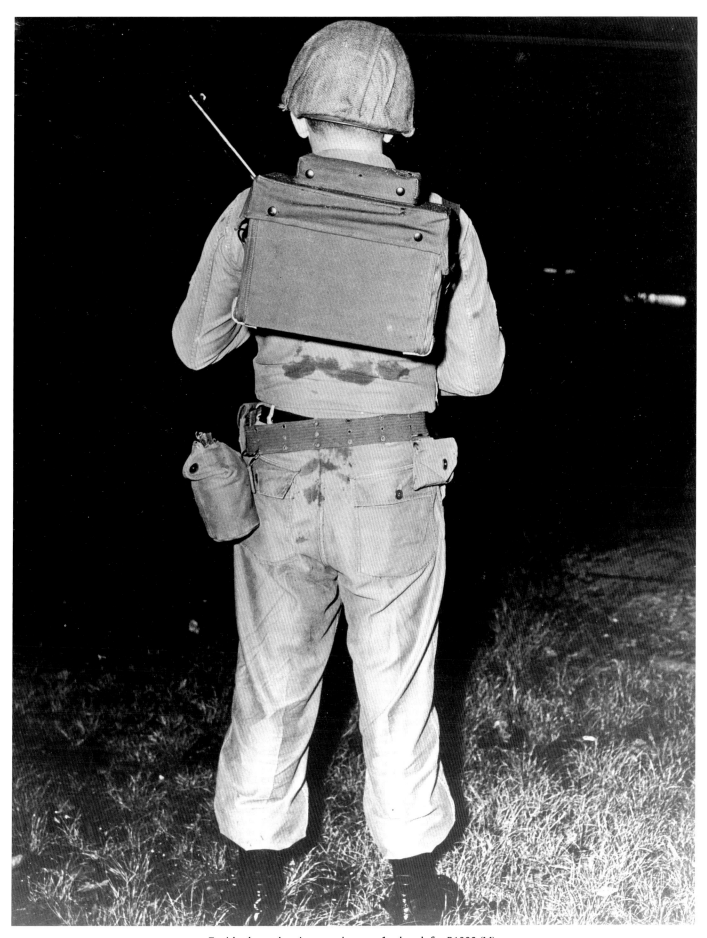

Zenith photo showing carrying case/backpack for R1000 (M).

Zenith photo showing another view of the R1000 (M) carrying case/backpack.

telligence Agency of the United States Government.

The other two transitorized military models were featured in the Zenith Annual Reports for 1963 and 1964. The first is referred to as the "Man Pack." The "Man Pack" was described in the 1963 report as follows: "Man Pack Radio Receiving System: An interesting example of a civilian product gone military is the lightweight Man Pack radio receiving and recording system developed and manufactured for the U.S. Marine Corps from the basic design of the famed Zenith Trans-Oceanic FM-AM short-wave portable receiver. Two Man Pack systems can be carried on a standard Marine pack-board. The system can tune and tape record AM and FM radio signals over a wide frequency range." The Man Pack was housed in a hard shell carrying case.

In the 1964 Annual Report, Zenith showed a second version of the Man Pack and now designated it as model ZX-5. This was another variation on the military "Trans-

Zenith photo showing backpack for model ZX-5.

Oceanic" design and this time the Annual Report stated: "The ZX-5 Man Pack, (descendant of Trans-Oceanic portable radio) has been tested in desert and jungle."

The military redesignated the ZX-5 radio as military radio number PR-15. The United States Marine Corps took delivery of one hundred radios from Zenith. This radio had continuous frequency coverage tunable from 550 Khz to 280 Mhz. Much of the engineering and special design work for the transistorized military "Trans-Oceanic" type radios was done by a team of engineers led by Dr. Robert Adler. Also on the team were Bill Counts, Jim Clark, Bill Van Slyck, Clarence Pipes, Ted Godowski, Ralph Clarke, Don Anderson, and Donn Abbott. Dr. Robert Adler also invented the first practical wireless remote control for television, another Zenith first.

It is unfortunate that the records for these receivers were lost and only this small amount of information has been saved. It is not known if any of these radios still exist. Locating one would certainly be the ultimate "find" for a Zenith "Trans-Oceanic" collector!

Zenith photo showing military type "Trans-Oceanic" model ZX-5.

Chapter 17

1966 AND BEYOND

An ever increasing flood of cheap radios from the Pacific rim began to cut deeply into Zenith's market share. Gone were the days when quality and improved performance were the driving forces in transistor radio design. Instead, low price controlled the future of the radio business, and only specialized radios received improvements in features and performance. The "Navigator" and "Trans-Oceanic" models continued to be built with traditional Zenith quality. In 1969 Zenith redesigned the "Trans-Oceanic." The all new Royal 7000 was an outstanding radio. New features such as manual gain control and BFO were standard. In addition, a band width switch and tuning meter made this set a true pleasure to operate. This Zenith "Trans-Oceanic" also included the new VHF weather band.

Details on the Royal 7000 and subsequent "Trans-Oceanic" models may be found in *The Zenith Trans-Oceanic: The Royalty of Radios,* written by John H. Bryant, AIA and Harold N. Cones, Ph.D.

Ultimately, even Zenith was forced to manufacture transistor radios in Asia in order to produce low-priced, small radios. Although these Zenith radios were of lesser quality than their predecessors, they were still excellent performers for the price. Most would easily outperform the competition.

CONCLUSION

The "Golden Age" of transistor radios, 1955-65, was characterized by increasing competition among manufacturers as well as consumer excitement surrounding the enjoyment of portable radios. Zenith's leadership during this era of the consumer electronics business was unparalleled, a tribute to the thousands of men and women who designed and built Zenith into the "Royalty of Radio."

My experience as a collector and enthusiast of Zenith transistor radios is a lifelong avocation that spans decades. As a result of my research at Zenith, I have happily found that as the company prepares for leadership in the digital technologies of tomorrow, the same spirit of innovation and focus on quality that epitomized the transistor radio's "Golden Age" continues at Zenith today.

While the Zenith Radio Corporation was not alone in driving innovation during that historic postwar period in consumer electronics, the company's commitment to quality set the highest of standards for the rest of the industry to follow. Indeed, the legendary Royal 500 and its successors, as well as the transistorized "Trans-Oceanics" and many other Zenith models detailed in this book, were the radios against which all others were measured.

ZENITH FACTORY SPEC SHEET PHOTOS: ESTIMATED VALUES

The prices listed here are solely the opinion of the author as of this writing. Market values are always determined by the condition of the set and the agreed on price between buyer and seller. The prices quoted are only to be used as a guide. Radios found with original paperwork and/or original box have added value. Radios found with complete gift ensemble have greatly increased value.

ZENITH ROYAL 40-G

Complete with custom carry case, earphone attachment and batteries in gift box.

6 TRANSISTOR
SHIRT POCKET RADIO

Estimated value if found complete and in good condition: $15.00.

ROYAL 20-G   *19.95*
Zenith
8 TRANSISTOR
VEST POCKET RADIO
COMPLETE WITH VINYL CARRYING LOOP, EARPHONE ATTACHMENT AND BATTERIES IN GIFT BOX.

• Powered by 8 Transistors
• Outstanding Audio Output
• Durable Cycolac Cabinet

Estimated value if found complete and in good condition: $20.00.

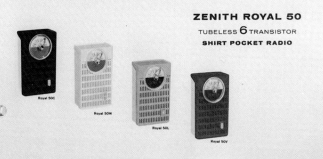

ZENITH ROYAL 50

TUBELESS **6** TRANSISTOR

SHIRT POCKET RADIO

ZENITH ROYAL 50H

TUBELESS **6** TRANSISTOR

SHIRT POCKET RADIO

Estimated value if found complete and in good condition: $20.00.
Estimated value if found complete and in good condition: $15.00.

Estimated value if found complete and in good condition: $20.00.
Estimated value if found complete and in good condition: $15.00.

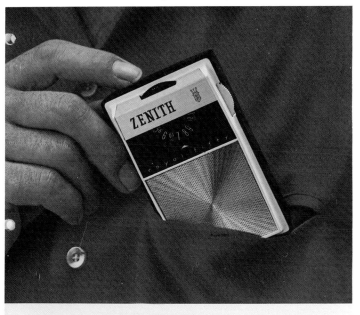

ZENITH ROYAL 50L

6 TRANSISTOR

SHIRT POCKET RADIO

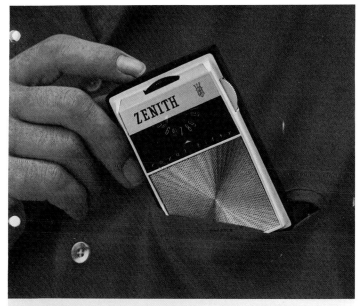

ZENITH ROYAL 50L-G

Complete with custom carry case, earphone attachment
and batteries in gift box.

6 TRANSISTOR

SHIRT POCKET RADIO

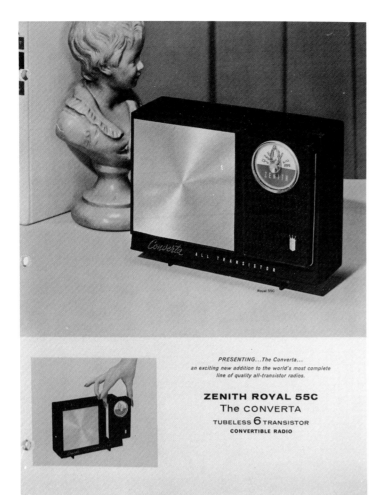

Estimated value if found complete and in good condition: $75.00.

Estimated value if found complete and in good condition: $15.00.

Estimated value if found complete and in good condition: $15.00.

ROYAL 59-1G

Zenith

**8 TRANSISTOR
SHIRT POCKET RADIO**

*COMPLETE WITH CUSTOM CARRY CASE,
EARPHONE ATTACHMENT AND
BATTERIES IN GIFT BOX*

- Zenith Quality Speaker
- Rugged Cycolac Cabinet
- Uses 2 Penlite Batteries

Estimated value if found complete and in good condition: $20.00.

ZENITH ROYAL 60

6 TRANSISTOR

SHIRT POCKET RADIO

Retail – $17.95
Dist. – $13.00

ZENITH ROYAL 80-G

Complete with custom carry case, earphone attachment and batteries in gift box.

8 TRANSISTOR

SHIRT POCKET RADIO

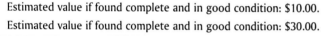

Royal 80W-G   Royal 80F-G   Royal 80Y-G

Estimated value if found complete and in good condition: $10.00.
Estimated value if found complete and in good condition: $30.00.

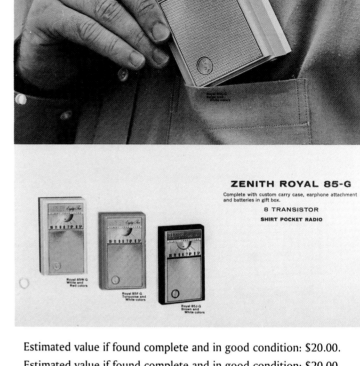

ZENITH ROYAL 85-G

Complete with custom carry case, earphone attachment and batteries in gift box.

8 TRANSISTOR

SHIRT POCKET RADIO

Royal 85W-G
White and
Red colors

Royal 85F-G
Turquoise and
White colors

Royal 85J-G
Brown and
White colors

Estimated value if found complete and in good condition: $20.00.
Estimated value if found complete and in good condition: $20.00.

Royal 90C

ZENITH ROYAL 90

TUBELESS 6 TRANSISTOR

SHIRT POCKET RADIO

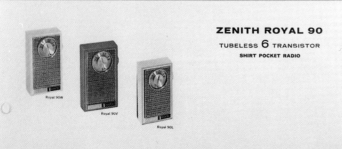

Royal 90W   Royal 90V   Royal 90L

ROYAL 100C

The Zenette
ZENITH ROYAL 100

TUBELESS ALL-TRANSISTOR

COMPACT POCKET RADIO

ROYAL 100F   ROYAL 100W   ROYAL 100J   ROYAL 100P

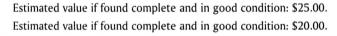

ZENITH ROYAL 125

TUBELESS 6 TRANSISTOR

SHIRT POCKET RADIO

WITH VERNIER TUNING

Estimated value if found complete and in good condition: $25.00.
Estimated value if found complete and in good condition: $20.00.

ZENITH ROYAL 130

TUBELESS 6 TRANSISTOR

SHIRT POCKET RADIO

WITH VERNIER TUNING

Estimated value if found complete and in good condition: $20.00.
Estimated value if found complete and in good condition: $25.00.

ZENITH ROYAL 130-G

Complete with custom carry case, earphone attachment
and batteries in gift box.

TUBELESS 6 TRANSISTOR

SHIRT POCKET RADIO

WITH VERNIER TUNING

ZENITH ROYAL 150

TUBELESS 6 TRANSISTOR

COMPACT POCKET RADIO

With Vernier Tuning

93

Estimated value if found complete and in good condition: $20.00.

ZENITH ROYAL 180-G

Complete with custom carry case, earphone attachment
and batteries in gift box.

8 TRANSISTOR

SHIRT POCKET RADIO

WITH SLIDE RULE DIAL

Estimated value if found complete and in good condition: $20.00.

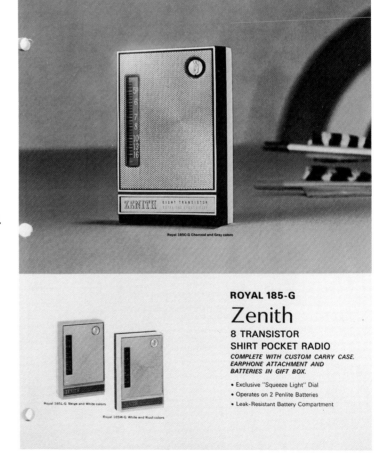

ROYAL 185-G

Zenith

8 TRANSISTOR
SHIRT POCKET RADIO

COMPLETE WITH CUSTOM CARRY CASE.
EARPHONE ATTACHMENT AND
BATTERIES IN GIFT BOX.

- Exclusive "Squeeze Light" Dial
- Operates on 2 Penlite Batteries
- Leak-Resistant Battery Compartment

Estimated value if found complete and in good condition: $45.00.

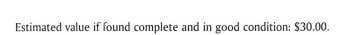

Estimated value if found complete and in good condition: $30.00.

ZENITH ROYAL 265

TUBELESS **6** TRANSISTOR

POCKET RADIO

WITH VERNIER TUNING

ROYAL 270-G   *19.95*

Zenith

8 TRANSISTOR

POCKET RADIO

COMPLETE WITH CARRY CASE, EARPHONE ATTACHMENT AND BATTERIES IN GIFT BOX

- Powerful Audio Output
- High-Impact Cabinet
- Uses 4 Penlite Batteries

Estimated value if found complete and in good condition: $40.00.

Estimated value if found complete and in good condition: $40.00.

Estimated value if found complete and in good condition: $25.00.

Estimated value if found complete and in good condition: $45.00.

From the AMERICANA Series...

The Statesman

ZENITH ROYAL 275

TUBELESS **7** TRANSISTOR

POCKET RADIO

WITH VERNIER TUNING

ZENITH ROYAL 280-G

Complete with deluxe carry case, earphone attachment and batteries in gift box.

TUBELESS **8** TRANSISTOR

POCKET RADIO

WITH VERNIER TUNING

34.95

ZENITH ROYAL 285-G

Complete with deluxe carry case, earphone attachment and batteries in gift box.

TUBELESS **8** TRANSISTOR

POCKET RADIO

With VERNIER TUNING

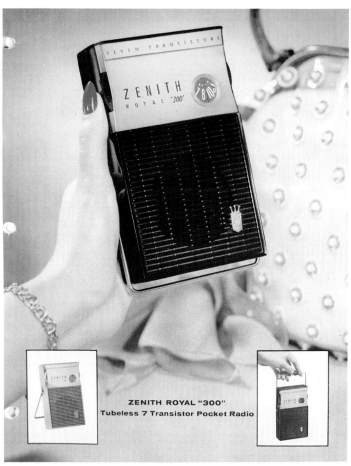

ZENITH ROYAL "300"
Tubeless 7 Transistor Pocket Radio

Estimated value if found complete and in good condition: $45.00.
Estimated value if found complete and in good condition: $70.00.

Estimated value if found complete and in good condition: $60.00.
Estimated value if found complete and in good condition: $60.00.

ZENITH ROYAL 400 TUBELESS 7 TRANSISTOR **POCKET RADIO**

featuring the amazing
New Exclusive **ZENITH**
EXTENDED RANGE
SPEAKER
that revolutionizes
pocket radio
tone quality.

Measures full 5" x 3"—the largest speaker of its kind ever put into this size radio. Develops more rich low notes and more clear high notes with greater acoustic power —the widest tonal range ever in pocket radio.

steep cone angle extends treble range

Powered by new, highly efficient ceramic magnet

larger cone area extends low range

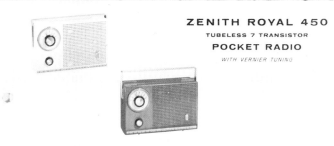

ZENITH ROYAL 450
TUBELESS 7 TRANSISTOR
POCKET RADIO
WITH VERNIER TUNING

Estimated value if found complete and in good condition: $65.00.

ZENITH ROYAL 475
World's Most Powerful Radio of its Size
TUBELESS **7** TRANSISTOR
"TABLE-TRAVEL" RADIO
WITH VERNIER TUNING

Estimated value if found complete and in good condition: $25.00.

ZENITH ROYAL 490L
TUBELESS **7** TRANSISTOR
PORTABLE RADIO

Estimated value if found complete and in good condition: $150.00.

Estimated value if found complete and in good condition: black, white, and burgundy, $100.00; beige, $300.00; pink, $350.00.

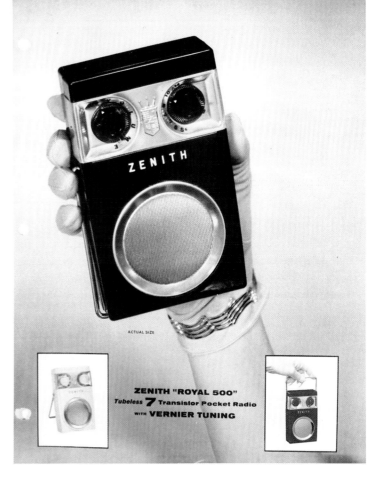

99

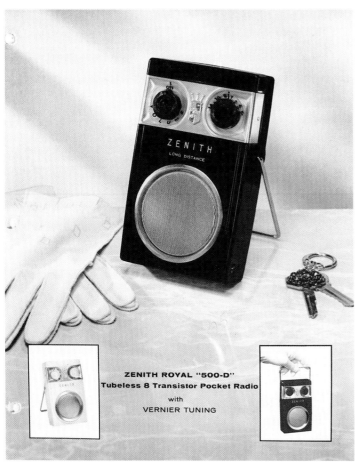

Estimated value if found complete and in good condition: $80.00.
Estimated value if found complete and in good condition: $75.00.

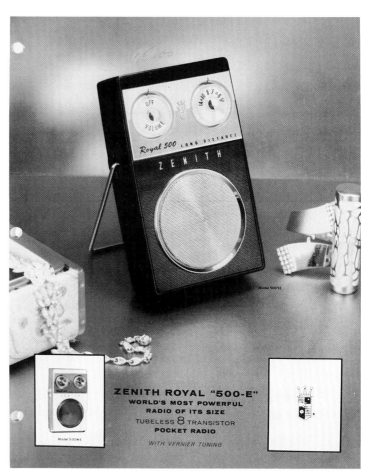

Estimated value if found complete and in good condition: $75.00.
Estimated value if found complete and in good condition: $50.00.

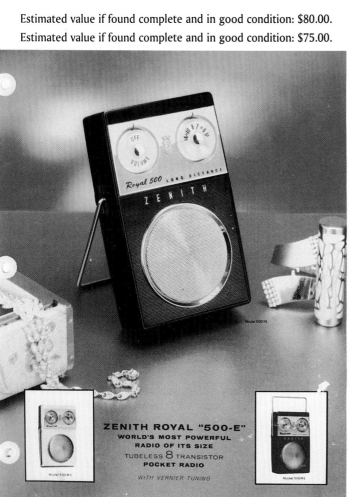

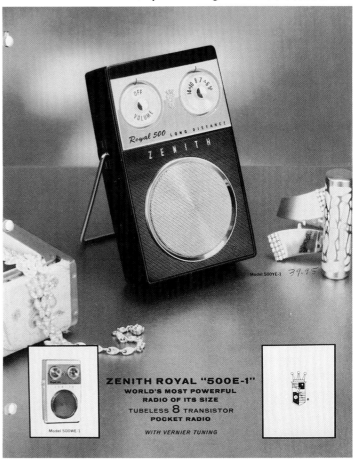

ZENITH ROYAL 500H DELUXE TUBELESS 8 TRANSISTOR **POCKET RADIO**

*The world's richest
tone quality in the
world's finest performing
pocket radio*

MODEL 500WH   MODEL 500GH

Estimated value if found complete and in good condition: $150.00.
Estimated value if found complete and in good condition: $40.00.

ZENITH ROYAL 500H-1 DELUXE TUBELESS 8 TRANSISTOR **POCKET RADIO**

*The world's richest
tone quality in the
world's finest performing
pocket radio*

MODEL 500WH-1   MODEL 500GH-1

Estimated value if found complete and in good condition: $100.00.
Estimated value if found complete and in good condition: $40.00.

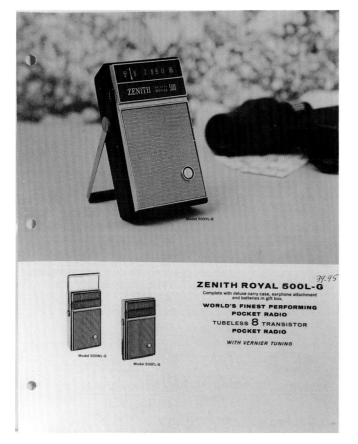

Model Royal 555C-G

Estimated value if found complete and in good condition: $250.00.

Model Royal 555W-G

Estimated value if found complete and in good condition: $250.00.

Estimated value if found complete and in good condition: $25.00.

ZENITH ROYAL 645
TUBELESS **6** TRANSISTOR
PORTABLE RADIO

Estimated value if found complete and in good condition: $25.00

ZENITH ROYAL 645L
TUBELESS **6** TRANSISTOR
PORTABLE RADIO

103

ZENITH ROYAL 650
TUBELESS 6 TRANSISTOR
PORTABLE RADIO

ZENITH ROYAL 670L
TUBELESS 6 TRANSISTOR
PORTABLE RADIO

Estimated value if found complete and in good condition: $25.00.
Estimated value if found complete and in good condition: $35.00.

Estimated value if found complete and in good condition: $35.00.
Estimated value if found complete and in good condition: $35.00.

From the AMERICANA Series...

The Independence
ZENITH ROYAL 675
TUBELESS 6 TRANSISTOR
PORTABLE RADIO

WITH VERNIER TUNING

ZENITH ROYAL 675LG
TUBELESS 6 TRANSISTOR
PORTABLE RADIO

WITH VERNIER TUNING

ZENITH ROYAL 700
TUBELESS **7** TRANSISTOR
PORTABLE RADIO

GENUINE LEATHER CABINET

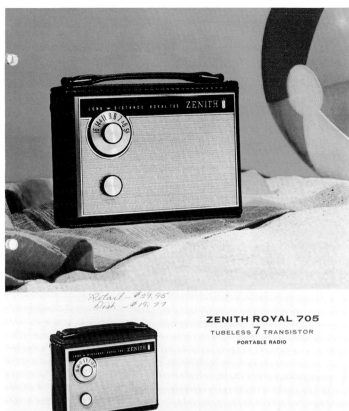

ZENITH ROYAL 705
TUBELESS **7** TRANSISTOR
PORTABLE RADIO

Estimated value if found complete and in good condition: $50.00.

Estimated value if found complete and in good condition: $30.00.

Estimated value if found complete and in good condition: $35.00.

Estimated value if found complete and in good condition: $30.00.

ZENITH ROYAL 710
TUBELESS **7** TRANSISTOR
PORTABLE RADIO

WITH VERNIER TUNING

ZENITH ROYAL 710LG
TUBELESS **7** TRANSISTOR
PORTABLE RADIO

WITH VERNIER TUNING

Estimated value if found complete and in good condition: $30.00.

ZENITH ROYAL 710LK
7 TRANSISTOR
PORTABLE RADIO

Estimated value if found complete and in good condition: $25.00.

ZENITH ROYAL 710M
7 TRANSISTOR
PORTABLE RADIO

Featuring • New Tone Control Switch •
• Provision For External AC Power Supply

ZENITH ROYAL 750
TUBELESS 8 TRANSISTOR
PORTABLE RADIO
GENUINE LEATHER CABINET

Estimated value if found complete and in good condition: $45.00.

Estimated value if found complete and in good condition: $35.00.

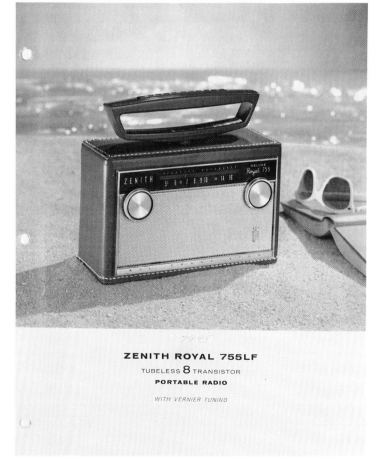

ZENITH ROYAL 755LF
TUBELESS 8 TRANSISTOR
PORTABLE RADIO

WITH VERNIER TUNING

ZENITH ROYAL 755LG

TUBELESS 8 TRANSISTOR

PORTABLE RADIO

WITH VERNIER TUNING

ZENITH ROYAL 755LK

8 TRANSISTOR

PORTABLE RADIO

*Featuring New Zenith "Battery-Saver"
That Can Double Battery Life . . .
Cut Battery Operating Costs in Half*

Estimated value if found complete and in good condition: $35.00.

Estimated value if found complete and in good condition: $25.00.

Estimated value if found complete and in good condition: $35.00.

Estimated value if found complete and in good condition: $65.00.

ZENITH ROYAL 755M *49.95*

8 TRANSISTOR

PORTABLE RADIO

*Featuring • New Tone Control Switch
• Provision For External AC Power Supply*

ZENITH *Royal "760"*
the NAVIGATOR

**Two-Band tubeless
all-transistor portable radio**

super-sensitive receiver for both standard broadcast
stations and weather service on government LF avia-
tion bands . . . ideal for fliers, yachtsmen, tourists,
outdoorsmen . . . and all who need outstanding reception of broadcast stations plus up-to-the-hour
weather reports, as well as long-range reception of
favorite programs on standard broadcast stations
at home . . . on the beach . . . or while traveling.

SELF-POWERED EMERGENCY NAVIGATIONAL AID FOR PLANES AND BOATS.

ZENITH *Royal "780YG"*

the NAVIGATOR.

SUPER-SENSITIVE · TWO-BAND
TUBELESS · 8 TRANSISTOR

PORTABLE RADIO

Super-sensitive receiver tunes standard broadcast and government LF weather-navigation bands . . . ideal for fliers, yachtsmen,
tourists, outdoorsmen . . . and all who need outstanding reception
of broadcast stations plus up-to-the-hour weather reports, as well
as long-range reception of favorite programs on standard broadcast stations at home . . . on the beach . . . or while traveling.

**SELF-POWERED, EMERGENCY, NAVIGATIONAL AID
FOR PLANES AND BOATS**

Estimated value if found complete and in good condition: $60.00.
Estimated value if found complete and in good condition: $70.00.

ZENITH *Royal "790Y"*

the SUPER-NAVIGATOR

SUPER-SENSITIVE · THREE-BAND
TUBELESS · 8 TRANSISTOR

PORTABLE RADIO

Super-sensitive receiver tunes the standard broadcast band,
FAA weather navigation stations on the 150 to 400 kc band and
Marine weather navigation and CAP stations on the 2 to 4-9 mc
marine band . . . ideal for fliers, sailors, yachtsmen, tourists, outdoorsmen . . . and all who need outstanding reception of up to
the hour weather reports, as well as long range reception of favorite programs on standard stations at home, in Europe or in the
Tropics . . . on the beach . . . or while traveling.

**SELF-POWERED EMERGENCY NAVIGATIONAL AID
FOR PLANES AND BOATS**

Estimated value if found complete and in good condition: $70.00.
Estimated value if found complete and in good condition: $75.00.

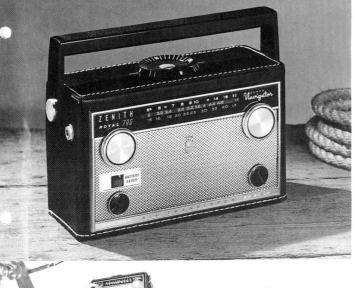

ZENITH *Royal "790YK"*

the SUPER-NAVIGATOR

SUPER-SENSITIVE · THREE-BAND
TUBELESS · 8 TRANSISTOR

PORTABLE RADIO

Super-sensitive receiver tunes the standard broadcast band, FAA
weather navigation stations on the 150 to 400 kc band and Marine
weather navigation and CAP stations on the 2 to 5 mc marine band
. . . ideal for fliers, sailors, yachtsmen, tourists, outdoorsmen
and all who need outstanding reception of up to the hour weather
reports, as well as long range reception of favorite programs on
standard stations at home, in Europe or in the Tropics . . . on the
beach . . . or while traveling.

**SELF-POWERED EMERGENCY NAVIGATIONAL AID
FOR PLANES AND BOATS**

ZENITH *Royal "790YK"*

the SUPER-NAVIGATOR

SUPER-SENSITIVE · THREE-BAND · TUBELESS · 8 TRANSISTOR

PORTABLE RADIO

Super-sensitive receiver tunes the standard broadcast band, FAA weather navigation stations
on the 150 to 400 kc band and Marine weather navigation and CAP stations on the 2 to 5 mc
marine band . . . ideal for fliers, sailors, yachtsmen, tourists, outdoorsmen . . . and all who
need outstanding reception of up to the hour weather reports, as well as long range reception
of favorite programs on standard stations at home, in Europe or in the Tropics . . . on the
beach . . . or while traveling.

SELF-POWERED EMERGENCY NAVIGATIONAL AID FOR PLANES AND BOATS

Estimated value if found complete and in good condition: $75.00.

the SUPER-NAVIGATOR

SUPER-SENSITIVE · THREE-BAND · TUBELESS · 8 TRANSISTOR
PORTABLE RADIO

Super-sensitive receiver tunes the standard broadcast band, FAA weather navigation stations on the 250 to 400 kc band and Marine weather navigation and CAP stations on the 2 to 5 mc marine band . . . ideal for fliers, sailors, yachtsmen, tourists, outdoorsmen . . . and all who need outstanding reception of up-to-the-hour weather reports, as well as long-range reception of favorite programs on standard stations at home, in Europe or in the Tropics . . . on the beach . . . or while traveling.

SELF-POWERED EMERGENCY NAVIGATIONAL AID FOR PLANES AND BOATS

Estimated value if found complete and in good condition: $250.00.

Zenith Tubeless **7** Transistor Portable Radio

ROYAL "800Y"
Ebony

Also available as Royal "800G"
in Silver Gray and Gobelin Blue

Estimated value if found complete and in good condition: $25.00.

Introducing...the world's finest performing compact
personal-size FM/AM portable transistor radio.

ROYAL 810
THE SYMPHONETTE
PERSONAL-SIZE FM/AM
TRANSISTOR RADIO

Complete with deluxe carry case,
earphone attachment and batteries
in beautiful gift box.

Estimated value if found complete and in good condition: $25.00.

Introducing...the world's finest performing compact
personal-size FM/AM portable transistor radio.

ROYAL 810-G
THE SYMPHONETTE
PERSONAL-SIZE FM/AM
TRANSISTOR RADIO

Complete with deluxe carry case,
earphone attachment and batteries
in beautiful gift box.

ZENITH FM/AM PORTABLE TRANSISTOR RADIO
The Symphony Model ROYAL 820

The World's Finest Performing FM/AM Transistor Radio

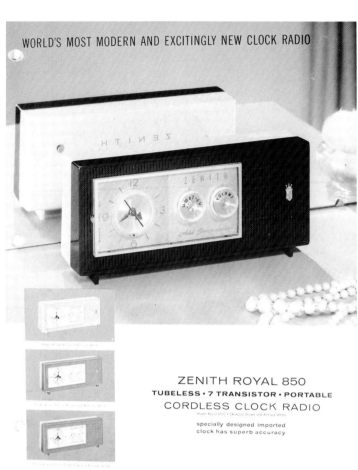

ZENITH ROYAL 850
TUBELESS · 7 TRANSISTOR · PORTABLE
CORDLESS CLOCK RADIO

Model Royal 850L · Charcoal Brown and Antique White

specially designed imported
clock has superb accuracy

Estimated value if found complete and in good condition: $25.00.
Estimated value if found complete and in good condition: $25.00.

Estimated value if found complete and in good condition: $65.00.
Estimated value if found complete and in good condition: $75.00.

ZENITH FM/AM PORTABLE TRANSISTOR RADIO
The Vocalaire Model ROYAL 880

The World's Finest Performing Personal Size FM/AM Transistor Radio

ZENITH ROYAL 900
tubeless **7** transistor
Cordless
Table/Portable Radio

ZENITH *Golden Triangle* Royal 950
ALL-TRANSISTOR CORDLESS CLOCK RADIO
Specially designed Swiss clock has superb accuracy

ZENITH *All-Transistor* TRANS-OCEANIC
STANDARD AND SHORT WAVE PORTABLE RADIO

9 transistors • smallest and lightest standard and band s...

Estimated value if found complete and in good condition: $250.00.
Estimated value if found complete and in good condition: $75.00.

Estimated value if found complete and in good condition: $150.00.
Estimated value if found complete and in good condition: $150.00.

WORLD'S MOST DISTINCTIVE FM/AM RADIO

ALL-TRANSISTOR

TRANS-SYMPHONY

ZENITH FM/AM PORTABLE RADIO-ROYAL 2000
FIRST AMERICAN MADE FM/AM PORTABLE ALL-TRANSISTOR RADIO

INTRODUCING...FM BROADCAST RECEPTION IN THE
ZENITH 12 TRANSISTOR TRANS-OCEANIC®
STANDARD BAND AND SHORTWAVE PORTABLE RADIO

THE ALL NEW ZENITH ROYAL 3000
POWERED TO TUNE IN THE WORLD...PROVIDES GLORIOUS FM FINE MUSIC ENTERTAINMENT

Estimated value if found
complete and in good
condition: $150.00.

Estimated value if found
complete and in good condition:
$200.00.

Estimated value if found
complete and in good
condition: $200.00.

Opposite page:
Zenith magazine ad, 1958.

ZENITH ADVERTISING AND PROMOTIONAL MATERIALS

Zenith puts a new level of performance into these all-transistor radios!

They all have something you've never heard before—Zenith tone, clear and true—they all bring in stations many others fail to reach. And they do it on low-cost flashlight batteries.

A. New! Cordless table radio—doubles as a portable! And you've never heard tone so rich and full in a transistor radio of this size. Has Zenith's own exclusive Wavemagnet® antenna built in. Only 4¹¹⁄₁₆ inches high, 7¾ inches wide, 3⅞₆ inches deep. In handsome black and white, green and grey, white and gold, the Royal 900, $69.95*.†

B. Pocket-size, but the tone is big! Plays in autos, trains, planes and boats . . . where less sensitive radios fail. Has Zenith's own exclusive Wavemagnet® antenna built in. Only 6⁹⁄₁₆" high, 4¹⁄₂" wide, 1³¹⁄₃₂" deep. In Cordovan Brown, Tahitian Coral, Glen Green or White, the Royal 200, $44.95*.†

C. Light and easy to take—everywhere! Only 3 lbs. 8¼ oz. Rated best of portable radios tested by leading independent testing laboratory. Full 4" speaker with Alnico 5 Magnet for clear, rich tone. In genuine top grain cowhide, the Royal 700, $69.95*.†

D. New! Super Sensitive Long Distance pocket radio . . . up to 300% more sensitivity from Zenith's own specially designed circuit. Precision Vernier Tuning insures quick pinpoint tuning accuracy. Even hard-to-get stations are easily located and tuned in. Unbreakable Nylon case. In maroon, white or ebony, the Royal 500D, $75.00*.†

†*Private listening attachments available at extra cost on all transistor model radios.*

A Zenith battery-operated portable is as necessary in your home as a flashlight in case of power failure caused by air raid or other emergency. Low-cost batteries for these Zenith all-transistor portables are available wherever flashlight batteries are sold.

ZENITH
THE QUALITY GOES IN BEFORE THE NAME GOES ON

New excitement in Zenith table models, too!

E. Wake up to rich, glorious Zenith tone quality! Multipurpose AC Clock Radio has a Zenith speaker with Alnico 5 Magnet. Wavemagnet® antenna. Sleep switch. Electric clock. Latest wrap-around styling has molded back. Model B515, AC only, in ebony, white, gold and white, two-tone blue, grey and white, $34.95*.

F. New! AC-DC Table Model Radio combines famous Zenith tone quality and new wrap-around styling. Beautifully molded back completes smart decorator look from every angle. Long-distance AM reception. Wavemagnet® antenna. Model B509 in gold and white, red and white, grey and white and two-tone green. $22.95*.

ZENITH RADIO CORPORATION, CHICAGO 39, ILLINOIS
Backed by 40 years of leadership in radionics exclusively
Also makers of television, high fidelity instruments and fine hearing aids
Manufacturer's suggested retail price. Prices and specifications subject to change without notice. (Transistor radio prices do not include batteries.)

Ad No. R-5811

Ad No. R-5811—L5084—Finished—1 page—9⅝ x 12⅛ in.—Esquire, Sept.; Look, Aug. 19, 1958
Printed in U.S.A.   Townsfolk, July, 1958—J889
Prepared by FOOTE, CONE & BELDING

Zenith showroom display from 1958 (Zenith "File Copy" photo).

Zenith photo of Fortnum & Mason store window display from 1959.

The perfect gift for your campus hero!

Zenith's new super-sensitive Royal 475!

Opposite page: Magazine ad from 1960 to introduce the new Royal 50.

Finest personal size all-transistor radio ever produced! It's a table radio, it's a travel radio—it's pure packaged power either way. Zenith's all-new Royal 475 outperforms any radio its size, delivers a sensational 250 milliwatts of undistorted power output on ordinary flashlight batteries! Deluxe quality components—tuned RF Stage with 3-gang condenser, Vernier tuning, inverse feedback—make possible unsurpassed sensitivity and tone. New "magna-lens" tuning control for pin-point station selection. And like all Zenith radios, it's quality-built in America by highly skilled, well-paid American workers. In black or beige polystyrene cabinet with snow-white metal grille. $49.95*.

Powered to tune in the world! A Zenith classic! Famous Trans-Oceanic® all-transistor portable radio receives both short wave and standard broadcasts—even navigation signals and FAA weather broadcasts. 9 supersensitive wave bands. Black Permawear covering with chrome and Roman Gold color trim. Royal 1000D, $275.00*†. Zenith's famous 8-band Royal 1000, $250.00*†.

ZENITH RADIO CORPORATION, CHICAGO 39, ILLINOIS. IN CANADA: ZENITH RADIO CORPORATION OF CANADA LTD., TORONTO, ONTARIO. The Royalty of television, stereophonic high fidelity instruments, phonographs, radios and hearing aids. 42 years of leadership in radionics exclusively.

ZENITH®

The quality goes in before the name goes on

Manufacturer's suggested retail price.   Prices and specifications subject to change without notice.   †Price includes batteries.

AD NO. R6067

Ad No. R6067—L9470—Finished—Page—7 x 10 in.—Sports Illustrated, November 14, 1960
New Yorker, November 19, 1960

Printed in U.S.A.

Prepared by FOOTE, CONE & BELDING

This ad was for late 1960 and was used to introduce the new Royal 475 for the 1961 model year.

All-new shirtpocket radio!
Only Zenith puts so much power and performance— such rich, full tone—into a radio so small! Only $29⁹⁵!*

Zenith's new all-transistor Royal 50 is smaller than a post card—yet no other radio of its size has ever been built to such exacting quality standards! It is quality-built in America by highly skilled, well-paid American workmen.

Plays up to 75 hours on 30¢ worth of batteries—almost twice as long as similar-sized radios that use special battery "packs" costing 4 to 5 times more! Zenith's new Royal 50 performs with remarkable sensitivity, tone and clarity, yet measures just 4⅜″ x 2¹¹⁄₁₆″ x 1¼″. Precision-built air dielectric type condenser provides full tuning accuracy. New nonbreakable, slim-styled cabinet in white or black solid colors; charcoal, beige or Chinese red two-tones with white. Private listening attachment optional at extra cost.

ZENITH RADIO CORPORATION, CHICAGO 39, ILLINOIS. IN
CANADA: ZENITH RADIO CORPORATION OF CANADA LTD., TORONTO, ONTARIO.
The Royalty of television, stereophonic high fidelity instruments, phonographs, radios and hearing aids. 42 years of leadership in radionics exclusively.
*Manufacturer's suggested retail price.
Price and specifications subject to change without notice.

ZENITH
The quality goes in before the name goes on

AD NO. R-6047

Copy No. R-6047—L9406—Finished—1 page—9⅜ x 12¼ in.—Life, October 24; Holiday, November;
Printed in U. S. A.   Esquire, November; Look, November 8, 1960
                    Prepared by FOOTE, CONE & BELDING

2 radios in 1!

It's a Zenith shirtpocket radio!

And it's a powerful Zenith table radio!

Converta ALL TRANSISTOR

WHAT A WONDERFUL NEW IDEA!

Announcing Zenith's new all-transistor Converta—a shirtpocket radio and a table radio—*all in one!* The shirtpocket radio detaches from the larger cabinet in a second —goes with you anywhere. It performs with remarkable sensitivity, tone and clarity—yet measures just $4\frac{3}{8}''$ x $2\ 11/16''$ x $1\frac{1}{4}''$. For indoor or patio listening, simply plug the shirtpocket radio into the larger cabinet, and *instantly* you have the big, full-room tone of a powerful cordless table radio! Operates on 2 low cost flashlight batteries. The Zenith Converta, Model Royal 55, handsome Duraperm cabinet in charcoal grey, only $44.95*.

Quality-built in America by highly skilled, well-paid American workmen

ZENITH

The quality goes in before the name goes on

ZENITH RADIO CORPO-
RATION, CHICAGO 39,
ILLINOIS. IN CANADA:
ZENITH RADIO CORPORATION OF CANADA
LTD., TORONTO, ONTARIO. The Royalty of
television, stereophonic high fidelity instruments,
phonographs, radios and hearing aids. 42 years
of leadership in radionics exclusively.
*Manufacturer's suggested retail price without batteries. Prices and specifications subject to change
without notice.

AD NO. R-6104

Copy No. R-6104—L9507—Finished—1 page—bleed—9⅜ x 12⅛ in.—Life, February 24; Esquire, March, 1961
Printed in U. S. A.

Prepared by FOOTE, CONE & BELDING

GREAT NEW ZENITH RADIO FOR OUTDOORSMEN!

New Zenith Royal 500-D all-transistor radio—so small it fits in your tackle box yet powered to perform where others fail

The world's most sensitive pocket radio. Up to 300% more sensitivity from Zenith's own specially designed circuits brings in distant stations loud and clear. Operates on flashlight batteries. Unbreakable Nylon case. Leather carrying case, optional at extra cost. In maroon, white or ebony. The Royal 500D, **$75.00***.

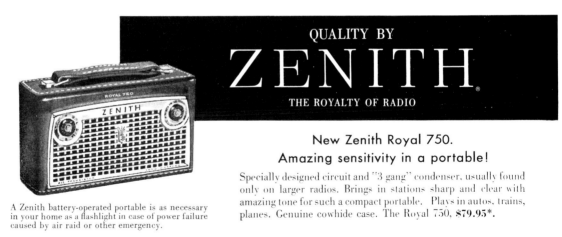

QUALITY BY

ZENITH®

THE ROYALTY OF RADIO

New Zenith Royal 750.
Amazing sensitivity in a portable!

Specially designed circuit and "3 gang" condenser, usually found only on larger radios. Brings in stations sharp and clear with amazing tone for such a compact portable. Plays in autos, trains, planes. Genuine cowhide case. The Royal 750, **$79.95***.

A Zenith battery-operated portable is as necessary in your home as a flashlight in case of power failure caused by air raid or other emergency.

ZENITH RADIO CORPORATION, CHICAGO 39, ILLINOIS
Also makers of Television, High-Fidelity Instruments and Fine Hearing Aids. Backed by 39 years of leadership in radionics exclusively.
Manufacturer's suggested retail price without batteries. Prices and specifications subject to changes without notice.

R-5804

Ad No. R-5804—L3717—Finished—1 page—7 x 10 3/16 in.—Sports Afield; Fisherman, June, 1958—J555
Printed in U. S. A.
Prepared by FOOTE, CONE & BELDING

May 1959 ad for
*Electrical
Merchandising,* a
retailers'
publication
about the sales
industry.

Making the best better

ZENITH'S
ROYAL 500D
World's most
powerful radio
of its size!

In 1955, Zenith introduced an all-transistor pocket radio that defied comparison—The Royal 500. It was the world's most powerful radio of its size, reflecting Zenith's lifelong policy not to compromise quality for price. Within a few months, the Royal 500 became the standard of excellence and performance in the industry. To make the best even better, Zenith, in 1957, added an untuned RF stage which increased signal sensitivity *four* times! Now, in 1959, Zenith's unique new inverted cone speaker gives the Royal 500D a richness of tone never before possible in so small a radio.

Making the best better is no new consideration at Zenith. For over 40 years, Zenith has maintained two policy principles regarding quality manufacture. First, to develop and produce

products of the highest quality. Second, and no less important, to strive constantly to improve products even though they rate best with millions. That's why consumers have learned to respect such features as the Zenith long distance radio chassis, the handsome, acoustically designed cabinets, the exclusive Wavemagnet° antenna that brings in even distant signals sharp and clear.

And Zenith is determined to continue making the best better; to continue making Quality a way of life; to continue applying the most stringent standards in the industry to all Zenith products.

This is our way of giving you, the Zenith dealer, not only more sales, but something more to sell than a price tag.

ZENITH RADIO
CORPORATION,
CHICAGO 39, ILL.

The Royalty of television, stereophonic
high fidelity instruments, phonographs,
radios and hearing aids. 40 years of
leadership in radionics exclusively.

ZENITH

*The quality goes in
before the name goes on*

Ad No. TR5912-R1—L9036TR—Finished—1 page—9 x 12 in—Electrical Merchandising, May, 1959
Printed in U. S. A.
Prepared by FOOTE, CONE & BELDING

Bracelet by Spaulding & Co., Chicago

Something you've never heard before

Zenith tone—clear and true in these *new* all-transistor radios

Now tune in Zenith tone that's vibrant and big in transistor radios that operate on flashlight batteries.

Even the smallest pocket size brings in stations others can't reach—with rich, full tone. Zenith high-fidelity sound engineers designed these all-new, all-transistor radios—with circuits that use only perfectly matched transistors.

QUALITY BY
ZENITH
THE ROYALTY OF RADIO

Ad No. R-5801—11x62—2 pages facing—ex. PR. 10 x 12¾ in.—Saturday Evening Post, May 24, 1958—
Printed in U S A
Prepared by Foote, Cone & Belding
J537

Ad No. R-5801

A. Everything is tiny but the tone! Has Zenith Wavemagnet Antenna built in—extra sensitivity that brings in distant stations strong and clear. In Pine Frost Green, white, maroon and ebony, the Royal 300 without batteries, $59.95*

B. Travels easy, travels light! Only 3 lbs, 8½ oz. Undistorted audio power output of 275 milliwatts. Precision Vernier Tuning makes fine tuning so much easier. Full speaker with Alnico 5 magnet for clear, rich tone. In genuine top grain cowhide, the Royal 700 without batteries, $69.95*

C. New! Long Distance! The world's most sensitive pocket radio. Up to 300% more sensitivity from Zenith's own specially designed circuit brings in distant stations loud and clear. Unbreakable Nylon case. In maroon, white or ebony. The Royal 500H without batteries, $75.00*

D. New! Cordless table radio—doubles as a portable! And you've never heard tone so rich and full in a transistor radio before. Measures only 4⅞ inches high, 7½ inches wide, 3⅜ inches deep. Handsome color combinations of black and white, green and grey, white and gold. The Royal 900 without batteries, $69.95*

E. Never before such sensitivity in a transistor radio! Specially designed circuit and 3-gang condenser, usually found only on larger radios, pulls in stations sharp and clear. Plays where others fail—in autos, trains, planes. Genuine top grain cowhide case. The Royal 730, without batteries, $79.95*

Powered to tune in the world! New Zenith all-transistor Trans-Oceanic—the smallest and lightest standard and band spread shortwave portable radio ever produced. Has 8 wave bands for world-wide broadcast, international short-wave, Marine, Weather and amateur reception. Handle lifts up to reveal telescopic Waverod Antenna (see illus.). Detachable Wavemagnet Antenna for reception on trains, planes, autos. The most magnificent radio ever built for travelers, sportsmen, yachtsmen—or anyone who appreciates the ultimate in radio. In black leather, chrome and Roman Gold trim, the Royal 1000 complete with batteries, $250.00*

ZENITH RADIO CORPORATION, CHICAGO 39, ILLINOIS.
Also makers of television, high-fidelity instruments and fine hearing aids.
Backed by 39 years of leadership in radionics exclusively

*Manufacturer's suggested retail price. Prices and specifications subject to change without notice

123

Distinctive Christmas idea!

Give Zenith–the gift of quality that can't in performance or styling!

PRIZED THE WORLD OVER, ZENITH PRODUCTS MAKE IDEAL

CHRISTMAS GIFTS. WHICHEVER ZENITH YOU CHOOSE IS TRULY

A GIFT OF QUALITY, UNQUESTIONABLY THE FINEST OF ITS KIND.

AND ZENITH QUALITY RADIOS START AS LOW AS $19.95.*

K. First time ever! Space Command* remote control tuning in portable TV! No wires, no cords, no batteries. Just touch a button to change channels, turn set on and off, adjust volume, even mute sound. Above, portable TV with Space Command 300. Side-mounted carrying handles, silver-brown vinyl-covered cabinet. 17" overall diagonal picture tube, 155 sq. inches of rectangular viewing area. Zenith Madrid, Model D2015, $249.95*.

L. True stereophonic high fidelity in a portable record playing instrument. Only Zenith gives you a giant 10" woofer in a self-contained stereo portable plus "pull-out" Zenith Radial Sound dual remote speakers which may be placed up to ten feet from the master cabinet. In briar brown color and white, the Zenith Operetta, Model SFD 111, $159.95*.

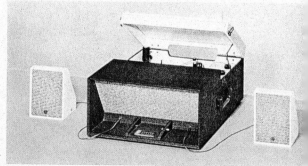

Ad No. R5932—L9149—Finished—2 page spread—19½ x 12⅛ in.—Life, November 30, 1959
Printed in U. S. A.
Prepared by FOOTE, CONE &·BELDING

Centerfold ad for November 30. 1959 issue of *Life* magazine.

124

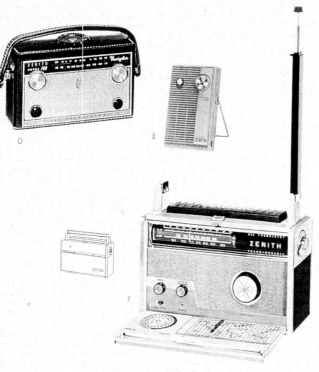

ZENITH QUALITY ALL-TRANSISTOR PORTABLE RADIOS
—MORE TONE, MORE POWER, MORE SENSITIVITY
FOR THEIR SIZE. THE WORLD'S FINEST—ZENITH RADIOS
PERFORM WHERE MANY OTHERS FAIL.

A. New design, new distinction, in the world's most powerful pocket radio of its size! First choice the world over. Up to 300% more sensitivity from Zenith's specially designed circuit. New improved speaker for richer, fuller tone. Nonbreakable nylon case in maroon, ebony color or two-tone combination of white and red. Zenith Royal 500E, $75.00*.

B. Big-toned, compact outdoor portable—rugged, but elegant. Easy-to-read slide-rule dial. Vernier tuning for pin-point station selection. Zenith quality speaker with heavy Alnico 5 magnet. Plays up to 350 hours on 6 low-cost batteries. In genuine cowhide, chrome plated grille. Royal 755, $79.95.*

C. World's most elegant cordless clock radio. The Golden Triangle, a sensitive long distance radio combined with imported clock of superb accuracy. Rotates at a touch, has three faces. Gold color, satin-finish panels, 17 Karat gold-flashed trim. Royal 950. $150.00.*†

D. World's most sensitive all-transistor 2-band (standard broadcast and long wave) portable! For pilots, boatsmen. Special FAA low-frequency, weather-navigation band, plus long-distance AM radio. Functions as self-powered stand-by navigation instrument. Superb tone. Genuine black leather case. Zenith Navigator, Royal 780, $99.95.*

E. Pocket-size—but with magnificent tone! Extra-strong audio output for high volume listening without annoying distortion. Wavemagnet° antenna receives even weak signals clear and strong. Scuff-resistant case in black, tan or white. The Zenith Americana, Royal 250, $39.95*.

F. World's most magnificent radio. Powered to tune in the world. Zenith's all-transistor Trans-Oceanic° radio—smallest and lightest standard and band spread short-wave portable radio made. Eight wave band Royal 1000, $250.00*†. Royal 1000D adds ninth band for FAA weather broadcasts, $275.00*†.

uplicated–

Long-distance, big-tone table radio. Full x 9″ speaker with heavy Alnico 5 magnet gives s long-distance AM table radio richer, fuller e. Three-gang condenser for increased signal sitivity. In two-tone decorator colors. AC/DC, del B615, $39.95*.

True high fidelity FM from two Zenith quality akers. Automatic frequency control assures ft-free FM reception. Long-distance AM ssis plus super sensitive FM radio. Rich, full e. Fine furniture cabinetry in maple, light or k walnut veneers or ebony color. Model C845, 9.95*.

Wake up to glorious FM music—with this ti-purpose FM/AM clock radio. Buzzer then s you 10 minutes after. Turns small kitchen liances on or off. Sleep switch turns off radio omatically. In black, white or green, Model 8, $79.95*.

emembers to call you even after you shut it This clock radio with Snooz-Alarm†† timer s you up to five times at 7 minute intervals r you shut off the alarm. Sleep switch turns ff automatically. Long distance AM chassis; remagnet° antenna. In pink, white or charcoal r. Model C624, $49.95*.

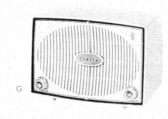

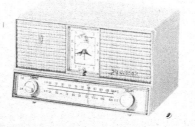

Amazing new speaker pours <u>room-size sound</u> from a <u>pocket-size radio!</u>

THE BIGGEST SPEAKER EVER PUT IN A POCKET RADIO LIES UNDER THE GOLDEN ( ) RING

THE NEW ZENITH ROYAL 500 DELUXE—MOST BEAUTIFUL POCKET RADIO EVER CREATED!

Created by Zenith, it revolutionizes pocket radio! You can't believe the big, rich, *room-size sound* you're hearing is actually coming from a *pocket-size radio*—because never before has there been a pocket radio with a speaker like this!

It's the revolutionary new Zenith exclusive "Extended-Range" speaker (figure A). Its *elliptical* design (figure B) gives it a much larger total speaker area than ordinary *round* pocket radio speakers. Furthermore, the voice-coil (figure C) is offset at the *top*—creating a much steeper cone angle. As a result, *for the first time*, you hear more clear high notes, more rich low notes—tone you've never heard from a pocket-size radio!

The "Extended-Range" speaker also features a radically new Ceramic Magnet (figure D). This *slim* new magnet allows a much larger speaker to be placed in a pocket radio than *ordinary* metal magnets do. This new speaker, combined with Zenith's advanced power output, gives you up to *4 times the volume* of other radios the same size!

Imagine—*room-size sound* from a *pocket-size radio! See it, hear* it—at your Zenith dealer's.

Eight transistors; non-breakable nylon case trimmed in Roman Gold color, comes in Ermine White, Ebony Color, Two Tone Ascot and Embassy Gray. Quality built in America by skilled American craftsmen. $60.00*.

ZENITH®

The quality goes in before the name goes on

ZENITH RADIO CORPORATION, CHICAGO 39, ILLINOIS. IN CANADA: ZENITH RADIO CORPORATION OF CANADA LTD. TORONTO, ONTARIO. The Royalty of television, stereophonic high fidelity instruments, phonographs, radios and hearing aids. 43 years of leadership in radionics exclusively. *Manufacturer's suggested retail price without batteries. Prices and specifications subject to change without notice.

Ad No. R6121

Copy No R-6121—L9611—Finished—page—9⅜" x 12⅛"—Holiday, Esquire, September, 1961
Printed in U.S.A.   *Prepared by* FOOTE, CONE & BELDING

September 1961 magazine ad for *Holiday* and *Esquire*.

One of a kind Christmas gift from Zenith!

New styling elegance! New exclusive speaker! Revolutionizes pocket radio!

The magnificent new Royal 500 Deluxe is the *can't miss* solution to your gift giving! It features the exclusive new Zenith "Extended Range" speaker, biggest *ever* in a pocket radio! You hear *more* clear high notes, *more* rich low notes—with up to *4 times* the volume of other radios the same size. You can hardly believe the big "*room size sound*" you're hearing is actually coming from this *pocket-size radio.* Hear this amazing new pocket transistor—then give it to the one you really want to please! Beautifully styled nonbreakable nylon case in white, ebony color, or two-tone grey, with Roman gold color trim. Eight transistors. Quality-built by skilled American craftsmen. $60*. Zenith quality pocket radios start at $26.95*.

New 5" x 3" speaker! Biggest ever in a pocket radio!

ZENITH RADIO CORPORATION, CHICAGO 39, ILLINOIS. IN CANADA- ZENITH RADIO CORPORATION OF CANADA LTD., TORONTO, ONTARIO. The Royalty of television, stereophonic high fidelity instruments, phonographs, radios and hearing aids. 43 years of leadership in radionics exclusively. *Manufacturer's suggested retail price without batteries. Prices and specifications subject to change without notice.

ZENITH

The quality goes in before the name goes on

R-6137

Copy No. R-6137—L9683—Unfinished—page—9⅜" x 12⅜"—Saturday Evening Post, November 25—Holiday, December, 1961. Printed in U.S.A.

Prepared by FOOTE, CONE & BELDING

RTK-D5578—9-19-61—B

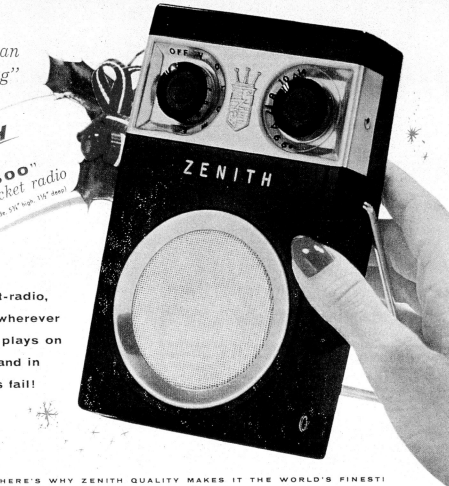

Opposite page:
Magazine ad for
December 11, 1956
issue of *Look*
magazine.

ZENITH NAVIGATOR®

all-transistor
2-band radio...
a self-powered
standby
navigation
instrument

PERFORMS WHERE OTHERS FAIL

Photos taken at Lake Atikameg, Manitoba, Canada

The world's most sensitive all-transistor 2-band (longwave and broadcast) portable. Powered to receive long distance reception of both range and standard broadcast stations even in many remote areas where others fail. No other all-transistor portable will keep you posted on weather conditions *all* along the line like the Zenith Navigator.®

Depend on the Navigator® for excellent reception in most airplanes. It homes accurately on broadcast and range stations with such a sharp null that pilots have dubbed it "The Poor Man's ADF." Solves To-From orientation without complicated range procedures. NAV switch eliminates AVC

to provide sensitive build-and-fade, easy LF range leg riding, and extremely sharp cones. Azimuth scale for quick reading of relative bearings.

Two ferrite plate-type antennas, tuned RF stage and 3-gang condenser give superior selectivity and sensitivity, and minimize broadcast station interference on LF band. Four-inch Alnico 5 speaker and push-pull audio give superior tone quality and adequate volume in most planes (earphones available at extra cost). Operates up to 350 hours on flashlight batteries. Has sturdy top grain cowhide leather cabinet. Only $99.95*.

See your nearest Zenith Dealer

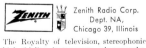 Zenith Radio Corp.
Dept. NA,
Chicago 39, Illinois

The Royalty of television, stereophonic high fidelity instruments, phonographs, radios and hearing aids. 40 years of leadership in radionics exclusively. *Manufacturer's suggested retail price without batteries.*

ZENITH
The quality goes in before the name goes on

Ad No. R5819

Zenith magazine ad
from 1958 for the
Royal 760.

Ad No. R5819—L6476—Finished—1 Page—7 x 10 in.—B&W—Flying Magazine, Skyways, December, 1958
Printed in U.S.A.

Prepared by FOOTE, CONE & BELDING

Zenith Radio Corporation
6001 DICKENS AVENUE
CHICAGO

L.C.TRUESDELL
VICE PRESIDENT
DIRECTOR OF SALES

November 14, 1958

Dear Zenith Dealer:-

Because of your enthusiastic reaction and your tremendous sales of Zenith quality transistorized radios such as the Royal 500D pocket radio and the Royal 1000 Trans-Oceanic radio, it gives me great pleasure to make an advance announcement of two NEW Zenith all-transistor products which offer you great new sales opportunities.

The attached specification sheets illustrate and describe Zenith's magnificent new GOLDEN TRIANGLE, Model 950, and Zenith's new Royal 850.

These new Zenith quality products present an entirely new concept in clock radios. They are 100% battery operated. They are cordless. They need no electric outlet. They can be operated and used anywhere a radio or clock operates.

I am sure you will agree that they are the most elegant, the most different, the most distinctive clock radios ever developed. Their smart appearance and their advance design virtually makes them conversation pieces and opens wide new opportunities for you in gift sales for discriminating customers.

Only Zenith with its 40 years of specialization in radionics could have developed such distinctively different products that are so new, so fresh, so attractive that there is nothing like them in the market.

But that is not all! You expect the finest quality from Zenith and these new Zenith products defy comparison!

In each of these new products, not only is the radio a full quality Zenith all-transistor radio, but the clock mechanism selected for these two new products is an excellent example of Zenith's determination to give you the world's finest quality.

page 2 continued on next page

November 14, 1958 letter to Zenith Dealers regarding new models.

In keeping with Zenith's rigid quality standards, Zenith researchers and engineers demanded the finest clock-mechanism obtainable and virtually searched to the ends of the earth to give you the most accurate, the most dependable, the most efficient clock-mechanism (called escapement type mechanisms) ever used in all-transistor clock radios.

After exhaustive testing of many clock mechanisms -- testing for accuracy, quietness, reliability, serviceability, the Zenith engineers finally specified fine imported clock mechanisms. Whereas, ordinary mechanisms have excessive time error in each 24 hours of operation, the mechanisms used in Zenith 850 and 950 are many times more accurate. Battery life of the clock mechanisms used by Zenith have almost twice the battery life -- up to one year -- as compared with others. Zenith's serviceability is good to excellent as compared with only fair in others.

Because these fine imported clock mechanisms are used to meet Zenith's rigid quality requirements, the Golden Triangle may be in short supply for a time inasmuch as the clock mechanisms are available only in limited supply. But you and your customers will find Zenith quality worth waiting for.

The quality story of the clock mechanism in these two superlative products is just another indication of Zenith's determination to give you the finest quality available -- something to sell besides a price tag.

I cannot put too much stress on the great opportunities for more sales for you using these two distinctive Zenith products.

The sale of the Zenith 500 and Royal 1000 has proved that there is a market for quality -- that your customers are willing to pay a fair price for the finest, for something distinctive and different ... something that others do not and cannot immitate.

We believe that these new Zenith products of quality, because of their styling, their design, their distinctive differentness and their operating efficiency, will give you important sales volume at a profit.

page 3 continued on next page

- 3 -

        Your Zenith distributor will be happy to show you
these truly exciting new Zenith products -- I am sure when you see them
you will agree that they are the world's most elegant and excitingly new
clock radios.

                                Very truly yours,

                                (signature) L. C. Truesdell

                                L. C. Truesdell

New elegance from Zenith!
The Golden Triangle — the new and unique
cordless, all-transistor clock radio

Wonderful gift idea! This exquisitely designed Zenith Golden Triangle is a new and distinguished concept in clock radios. It's a sensitive Zenith all-transistor radio—it's a superbly accurate imported clock. Use it anywhere in your home—it's cordless, no electric outlet needed. Operates on low-cost flashlight batteries. Only 8¾″ high, 5⅞″ wide. Gold color satin-finish side panels, 17 karat gold-flashed trim, the Zenith Royal 950, is priced at $150.*

To meet Zenith's rigid quality requirements, a fine imported clock movement of superb accuracy has been used in the Golden Triangle. The supply of these clock movements is limited and for that reason you may find the Golden Triangle in short supply but we believe you'll find it is worth waiting for.

The Golden Triangle rotates at a touch, turns three handsome faces to the world—a radio dial, a clock, a trim speaker grille.

R 5818

ZENITH RADIO CORPORATION, CHICAGO 39, ILLINOIS
The Royalty of television, stereophonic high fidelity instruments, phonographs, radios and hearing aids. 40 years of leadership in radionics exclusively. *Manufacturer's suggested retail price. Price and specifications subject to change without notice.

ZENITH

*The quality goes in
before the name goes on*

Amazing new speaker pours room-size sound from a pocket-size radio!

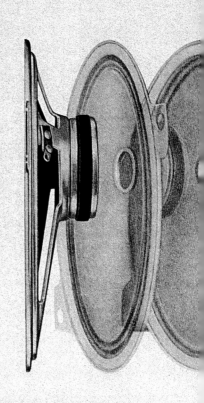

Announcing the fabulous new Zenith Royal 500 Deluxe!

It revolutionizes pocket radio! You can't believe the big, rich, *room-size sound* you're hearing is actually coming from a *pocket-size radio*—because there's never been a pocket radio with a speaker like this! It's the fabulous new Zenith Royal 500 Deluxe, with the exclusive "Extended-Range" speaker (figure A). This speaker's *elliptical* design (figure B) gives it a much larger total area than ordinary *round* pocket radio speakers. Furthermore, the voice-coil (figure C) is offset at the *top*—creating a much *steeper* cone angle. As a result, *for the first time*, you hear more clear high notes, more rich low notes—tone you've never heard from a pocket-size radio! The "Extended-Range" speaker also features a radically n Ceramic Magnet® (figure D). This *slim* new magnet allo a much larger speaker to be placed in a pocket radio th *ordinary* metal magnets do. This new speaker, combi with Zenith's advanced power output, gives you up t *times the volume* of other radios the same size! Imagin *room-size sound* from a *pocket-size radio!* You have to it, hold it, hear it, to believe it. Hear it at your Zer dealer's now! Eight transistors; non-breakable nylon c trimmed in Roman Gold color. In Ermine White, Eb Color, Two Tone Ascot and Embassy Gray. Quality b in America by skilled American craftsmen. $75.00*.

Another great achievement, a new styling trend, from Zenith — world leader in radio for over 43 yea

Copy No. R6120—L9601—Finished—2 facing pages—19½" x 12½"—Life, June 23, 1961
Printed in U.S.A. *Prepared by* FOOTE, CONE & BELDING
RTK·D1756—5-9-61—E

Centerfold ad for July 28, 1961 issue of *Life* magazine.

Elegance in design

UNDER THE GOLDEN RING ◯ LIES THE BIGGEST SPEAKER
EVER PUT IN A POCKET RADIO!

Zenith magazine ad, 1965.

NOW ZENITH HARNESSES THE SUN TO POWER THIS REVOLUTIONARY NEW SOLAR RADIO!

From advanced Zenith research comes the Sun Charger—the most remarkable radio under the sun.

The Sun Charger's solar cells produce power from sunlight . . . power this amazing Zenith transistorized radio stores in its rechargeable batteries to make it play indoors or out, night or day.

The Sun Charger virtually eliminates battery replacement, and if you live north of the Arctic Circle, where the sun doesn't shine six months of the year, don't worry. The Sun Charger can be plugged into the wall to play or charge during those long winter nights.

See and hear the revolutionary new Zenith Sun Charger soon . . . now at your Zenith dealer's.

ZENITH

The quality goes in before the name goes on

ZENITH SUN CHARGER ROYAL 555
55 60 · 70 80 90 · 120 160
ALL TRANSISTOR

SMART, DISTINCTIVE, COMPACT STYLING...uses less than one square foot of counter space.

Here is a striking, extremely attractive counter display which ties in perfectly with the high quality styling of the Zenith Royal "500" Pocket Radio. This De Luxe showcase is made of top grade wood and heavy duty, beveled edge plate glass and tapers smartly from top to bottom. Hidden incandescent bulb sheds soft direct light on radios. Hinged door on back has sturdy lock to prevent pilferage -- key is supplied. Golden flock background provides rich, attention-getting contrast for Maroon and Ebony colors of radios.

Shipped in special container.   Dimensions: $13\frac{3}{4}$" high, 18" wide, $7\frac{1}{2}$" deep.

ORDER BY FORM NO. R-6265 FROM YOUR ZENITH DISTRIBUTOR

Zenith promotional photo showing counter top transistor radio showcase for first series Royal 500.

Form No. R-6291

NEW DELUXE ZENITH "ROYAL 500" ILLUMINATED SHOWCASE DISPLAY (R-7086) LETS YOU DISPLAY COMPLETE LINE OF WORLDS FASTEST SELLING RADIO IN LESS THAN 1 SQUARE FOOT

This smartly styled illuminated showcase uses less than one-square foot of counter space. Here is an extremely attractive, rich looking showcase that lets you display the Zenith Royal 500 in all colors. The showcase is constructed of top grade wood and heavy duty, beveled edge glass. A hidden incandescent lamp sheds soft light on radios. Soft, golden flock background imparts rich contrast for various colors of Royal 500. Showcase furnished with bulb, socket, electric cord and plug.

Shipped in special container. Showcase measures 18½" high, 18" wide, 7½" deep.

ORDER AS FORM R-7086 FROM YOUR ZENITH DISTRIBUTOR

Zenith promotional photo showing counter top transistor radio showcase for second series Royal 500.

Form No. R-7091

138

NEW!! SENSATIONAL! ZENITH *"TWIRL-N-SELL"* TRANSISTOR RADIO SHOWCASE LETS YOU DISPLAY COMPLETE SELECTION OF ZENITH TRANSISTOR RADIOS IN ONLY 1½ FEET OF COUNTER SPACE.

**IT SWIVELS
3 SIDED**

**PLASTIC WINDOWS
SLIDE UP**

PILFER PROOF . . . DISPLAYS 12-18 TRANSISTOR RADIOS

Designed, styled to enable Zenith Dealers to display in Super Market Fashion a complete selection of Zenith All Transistor Radios yet use a minimum of counter space. This 3 Sided Transistor Radio selling department swivels at a touch of a finger to reveal any of the 3 sides. 3 sided header locks plastic windows in place to prevent pilferage . . . unlock header and clear plastic windows slide up for easy radio accessibility. Showcase comes equipped with 3 keys. Packed in one carton.

ORDER FROM YOUR ZENITH DISTRIBUTOR AS R-9007

FORM NO. R-9008

Zenith promotional photo showing "Twirl-N-Sell" transistor radio showcase.

ALL NEW! JEWELER TYPE! TRANSISTOR RADIO SHOWCASE
LIFTS PRODUCTS OFF FLOOR FOR EASY SHOPPING
!holds up to 35 Zenith Transistors!

pilfer proof!

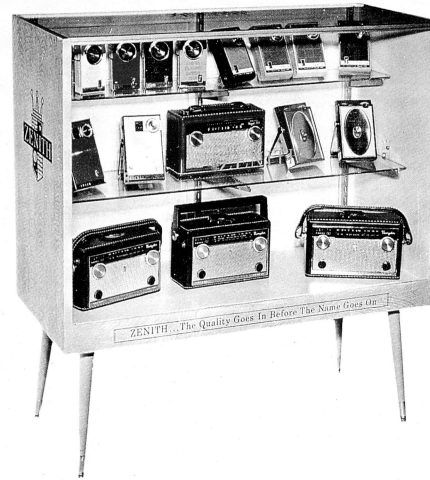

rear sliding doors!

Zenith promotional photo
showing Jeweler type
transistor radio showcase.

This all new Deluxe Zenith transistor radio display showcase makes it possible for improved exposure of Zenith radios for extra sales. Display stands 38″ high, 38″ wide and 16″ deep, includes 2 glass shelves and brackets. Finished in natural birch with cream colored interior. Built in lock for rear sliding doors with 2 keys. Shipping weight approximately 70 lbs.

ORDER FROM YOUR DISTRIBUTOR FORM NO. R-1089

ALL NEW ZENITH TRANSISTOR RADIO SHOWCASE
HIDEAWAY STORAGE SPACE!!!   SPECIAL GIFT BOX SHELF!!!

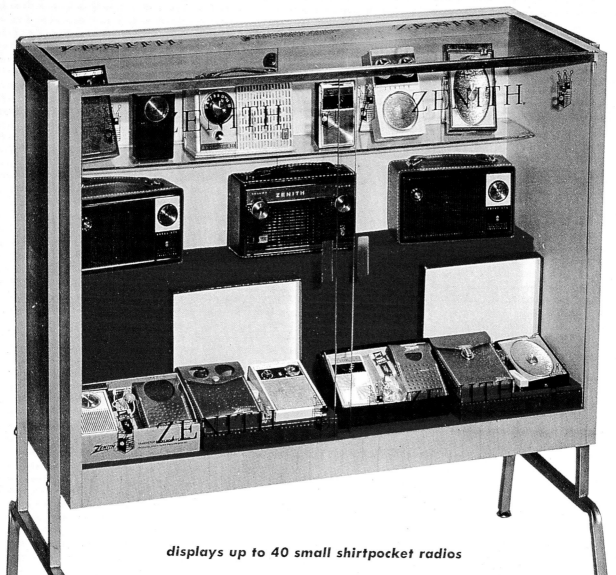

displays up to 40 small shirtpocket radios

This deluxe glass-type showcase has birchwood finish and cream-color interior. Front opening. Sliding glass doors. Includes lock for "pilfer-proof" usage. Sliding doors on back also providing access to storage space below the shelf area. Red velvet shelves with special shelf for gift box package display. Dimensions: 37″ wide, 16½″ deep, and 37″ high. Sturdy ¾″ square steel tube legs finished in gold provides rigid support.

Zenith promotional photo showing deluxe glass-type showcase.

(Chrome plated fluorescent fixture optional at extra cost)

Approximate shipping weight: 95 lbs.

ORDER FROM YOUR DISTRIBUTOR FORM No. R3216

FORM NO. R-3217

PRINTED IN U.S.A.

NEW *ZENITH* ROYAL 500D DISPLAY - GIFT BOX

PROVIDES JEWEL LIKE SETTING FOR WORLD'S FINEST

ALL TRANSISTOR POCKET RADIO

IDEAL FOR DISPLAY OF ROYAL 500D!
DISTINCTIVE GIFT BOX!

BEAUTIFUL, DISTINCTIVE DISPLAY-GIFT BOX ADDS EVEN GREATER APPEAL TO ZENITH
ROYAL 500D!   THE BOX IS OF HEAVY BOARD COVERED IN RICH BLACK AND STRIKING
GOLD WITH CONTRASTING RED FABRIC RIBBON. ZENITH CREST ON COVER IS OF ACTUAL
METAL IN GOLD COLOR. INTERIOR OF COVER IS STRIKING GOLD WITH ZENITH PRINTED
IN BLACK. ROYAL 500D RESTS IN A SETTING OF RICH WHITE FABRIC WHICH PROVIDES
JEWEL LIKE SETTING.   SIZE 5¼" wide: 1¾" high, 8¼" deep.

ORDER FROM YOUR ZENITH DISTRIBUTOR BY FORM NO. R-8139

Form No. R-8156

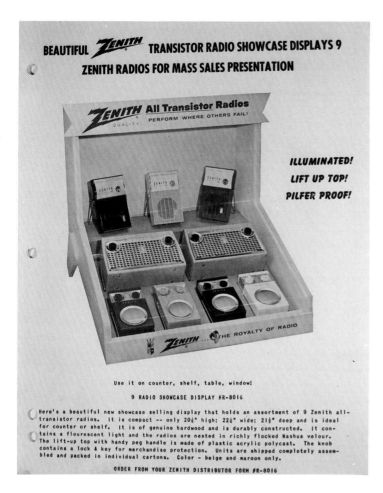

BEAUTIFUL ***Zenith*** TRANSISTOR RADIO SHOWCASE DISPLAYS 9
ZENITH RADIOS FOR MASS SALES PRESENTATION

Zenith All Transistor Radios
QUALITY   PERFORM WHERE OTHERS FAIL!

ILLUMINATED!
LIFT UP TOP!
PILFER PROOF!

Zenith ... THE ROYALTY OF RADIO

Use it on counter, shelf, table, window!
9 RADIO SHOWCASE DISPLAY #R-8016

Here's a beautiful new showcase selling display that holds an assortment of 9 Zenith all-transistor radios. It is compact -- only 20½" high; 22½" wide; 21½" deep and is ideal for counter or shelf. It is of genuine hardwood and is durably constructed. It contains a flourescent light and the radios are nested in richly flocked Nashua velour. The lift-up top with handy peg handle is made of plastic acrylic polycast. The knob contains a lock & key for merchandise protection. Units are shipped completely assembled and packed in individual cartons. Color - beige and maroon only.

ORDER FROM YOUR ZENITH DISTRIBUTOR FORM #R-8016

Zenith promotional photo showing counter top transistor radio showcase.

Zenith promotional photo showing deluxe transistor radio showcase.

ZENITH DELUXE TRANSISTOR RADIO SHOWCASE

This beautiful, deluxe showcase fixture enables you to display the entire line of Zenith quality transistor radios in keeping with the finest of store decors. Measures 22" deep; 48" long; 38" high. Plate glass ends, front and top. Base exterior and other wood trim in oak wood in limed oak finish. 2 adjustable glass shelves. One 6" the other 10". Two handy storage drawers. Inside of case illuminated by fluorescent fixture with on/off switch; built in ballast box; electrical outlet; lock to secure sliding doors; ventilated to dispense any heat. Weight 170 lbs.; crated weight 200 lbs.

ORDER FROM YOUR ZENITH DISTRIBUTOR AS FORM R-9227

Opposite page:
Zenith promotional photo showing Royal 500D distinctive gift box.

143

NEW *Zenith* POCKET RADIO

MERCHANDISER GIFT PACKAGE
FOR EVERY GIFT GIVING OCCASION!
ALL NEW QUALITY DESIGN --- RICH, BEAUTIFUL COLORS!

TRANSPARENT ACETATE COVER
LETS PROSPECTS SEE WHAT'S INSIDE

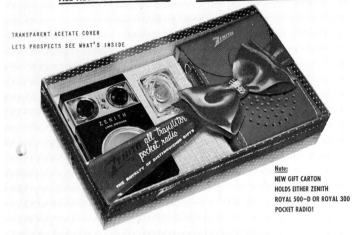

Zenith promotional photo showing Royal 500D gift carton.

Note:
NEW GIFT CARTON
HOLDS EITHER ZENITH
ROYAL 500-D OR ROYAL 300
POCKET RADIO!

DISPLAY IT ON THE COUNTER! DISPLAY IT IN THE WINDOW!
GET MORE POCKET RADIO GIFT SALES ALL YEAR LONG!

The distinctive, quality design of this new Zenith pocket radio Gift Package will add further gift appeal to the new Zenith Royal 500-D and Royal 300 pocket radios. The new Zenith gift carton has been designed so that it does not tie-in with any specific gift season---it's ideal for EVERY gift giving occasion. The combination of the rich "gold" and bright red colors will attract attention to the gift package when you display it in your store.

THE CARTON IS DESIGNED TO HOLD:

1 - ZENITH ROYAL 500-D OR ROYAL 300 POCKET RADIO
1 - CARRYING CASE FOR ZENITH ROYAL 500-D or ROYAL 300
1 - EARPHONE ATTACHMENT

Batteries should be inserted in radio when placing radio and accessories in carton. This new carton will also help you move more pocket radio accessories. The acetate cover adds to the quality "feel" of the package while providing protection from pilferage. The carton is made of sturdy board and each is shipped with a sleeve to protect the acetate cover..

CARTON SIZE: 2½" high; 11⅛" wide; 7" deep.   COLORS: GOLD, RED, WHITE, BLACK.

ORDER FROM YOUR ZENITH DISTRIBUTOR BY FORM NUMBER R-8046

NEW WINDOW DISPLAY
FOR WORLD'S MOST ELEGANT CLOCK RADIOS.
LIGHT, ACTION, AND LUXURIOUS VELOUR BACKGROUND HELP ZENITH DEALERS SPOTLIGHT ATTENTION ON ZENITH "GOLDEN TRIANGLE" AND ROYAL 850 . . . The world's most elegant All-Transistor, Cordless Clock Radios.

Zenith promotional photo featuring "Golden Triangle" and Royal 850.

This beautiful display was designed for use in dealer window to help focus attention on these revolutionary new Clock Radios from Zenith. The Zenith "Golden Triangle" revolves on a turntable to allow prospects to see all three sides. Background is of rich, luxurious and regal velour material in deep burgundy color. Display is illuminated for use at night to draw even more customer attention. Display holds "Golden Triangle" and two ROYAL 850's. Dimensions: 26" High, 27" Wide, 12" Deep. Individually packed.

ORDER FROM YOUR ZENITH DISTRIBUTOR AS R-8259

144

Zenith promotional poster featuring Royal 500D.

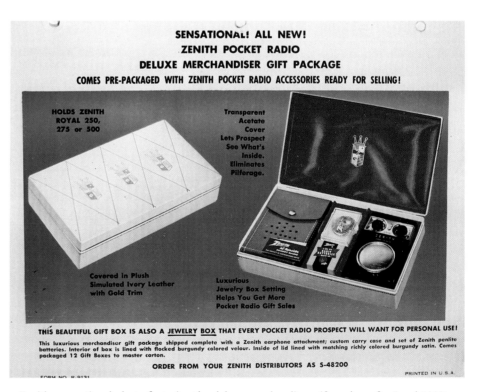

Zenith promotional photo featuring the deluxe merchandiser gift package for Royal 500D.

Zenith promotional photo featuring "Made In America" advertising.

Opposite page:
Zenith promotional photo featuring "Frame the Quality" display for Zenith Royal 500H.

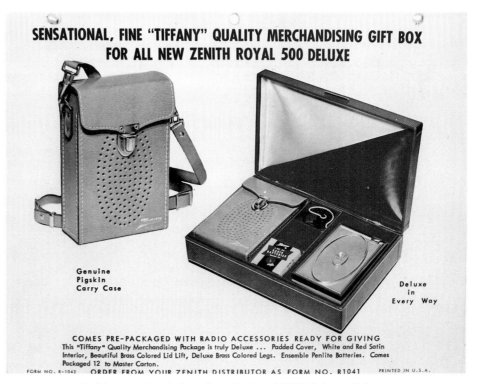

Zenith promotional photo featuring Royal 500H deluxe gift box.

NEW "FRAME THE QUALITY" DISPLAY FOR NEW ZENITH ROYAL 500 DELUXE LETS YOU GET BIG EXPOSURE IN MOST DELUXE SETTING FOR THIS SENSATIONAL NEW RADIO! COMES COMPLETELY SET UP!

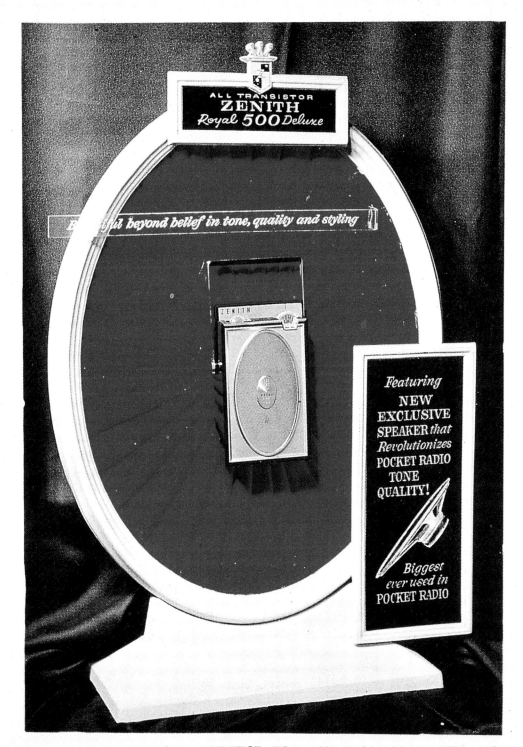

DISPLAY IS COMPACT! PERFECT FOR WINDOW/COUNTER USE!

This beautiful display is semi-permanent. It puts this new, sensational Radio in the setting it deserves. The Display needs no further embellishments . . . it is so attractive in itself and it tells, graphically, the customer that this Radio is world's finest Quality, Performance and Styling.

ORDER FROM YOUR ZENITH DISTRIBUTOR AS FORM NO. R1103

FORM NO. R1102

PRINTED IN U.S

ZENITH DEALER COUNTER/WINDOW DISPLAY
FOR ZENITH ROYAL 555 SUN CHARGER RADIO

Zenith promotional photo featuring Zenith display for Royal 555 "Sun Charger."

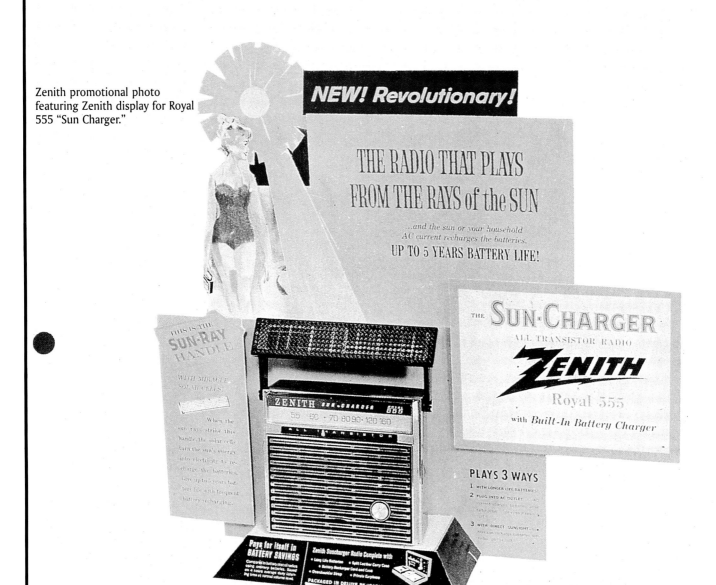

ATTRACTIVE! SELLS THE BENEFITS! ATTENTION GETTING!

Display incorporates a locking device that secures the radio to the display to prevent pilferage. Copy tells the big customer benefits of this new sensational radio. Display is very easy to set up.

ORDER FROM YOUR ZENITH DISTRIBUTOR AS FORM NO. R5134

FORM NO. R5135

PRINTED IN USA

DRAMATIC *ZENITH* DEALER ROYAL 1000 COUNTER/WINDOW DISPLAY THAT SPOTLIGHTS "WORLDS MOST MAGNIFICENT RADIO" IN A MAGNIFICENT HIGH QUALITY, HIGH FASHION SETTING

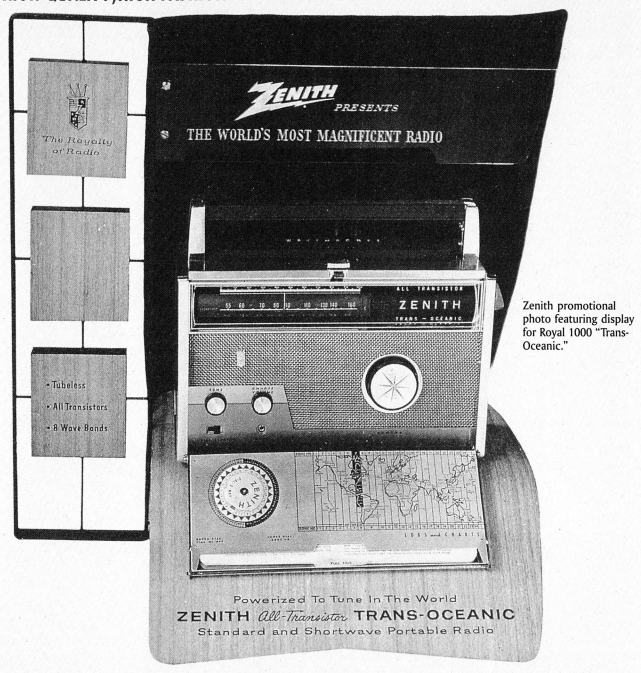

Zenith promotional photo featuring display for Royal 1000 "Trans-Oceanic."

ILLUMINATED TO GIVE EDGELIGHTING EFFECT

DESIGNED TO BE IN KEEPING WITH THE ZENITH HIGH QUALITY ROYAL 1000 ALL TRANSISTOR TRANS OCEANIC RADIO. ROYAL 1000 SITS ON WOOD PLATFORM OF BLEACHED GRAINED MAHOGANY FINISH. SIDE COPY PANELS ALSO IN SAME FINISH. BEAUTIFUL ROYAL BLUE SILK VELVET PROVIDES RICH BACKGROUND. SOCKET FOR LIGHT BULB HIDES BEHIND RADIO AND PROVIDES EDGELIGHTING EFFECT TO LUCITE HEADER SIGN AND CAST SOFT ILLUMINATION ON VELVET BACKGROUND MATERIAL. ENTIRE DISPLAY WEIGHS 8½ LBS. CAN BE ASSEMBL-ED IN A MATTER OF MINUTES. COMES INDIVIDUALLY PACKED.

ORDER AS R-7379 FROM YOUR ZENITH DISTRIBUTOR

Form No. R-7381

149

Zenith promotional photo featuring multi-band radios.

ZENITH DEALER
3 SET MULTI-BAND RADIO DISPLAY

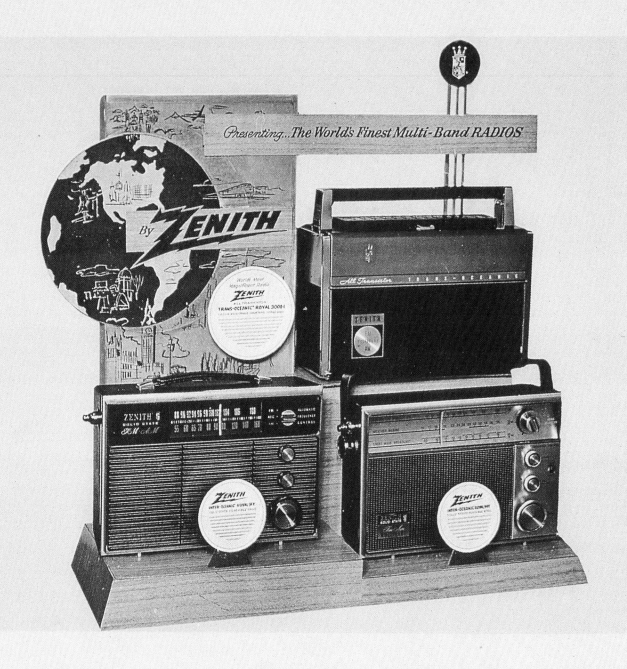

PERFECT FOR COUNTER OR WINDOW USE!

This very attractive atmosphere and feature selling display enables you to focus customer attention on World's Most Magnificent Radios . . . the Zenith Models Royal 3000-1, Royal 914 and Royal 944. Display sets up in minutes. Outstanding construction for long lasting display use.

ORDER FROM YOUR ZENITH DISTRIBUTOR AS FORM No. R-6088

FORM No. R-6089-566   PRINTED IN U. S. A.

HIGH QUALITY, ALL NEW CARRY CASE FOR
ZENITH ROYAL 1000 AND ROYAL 3000-1 RADIOS

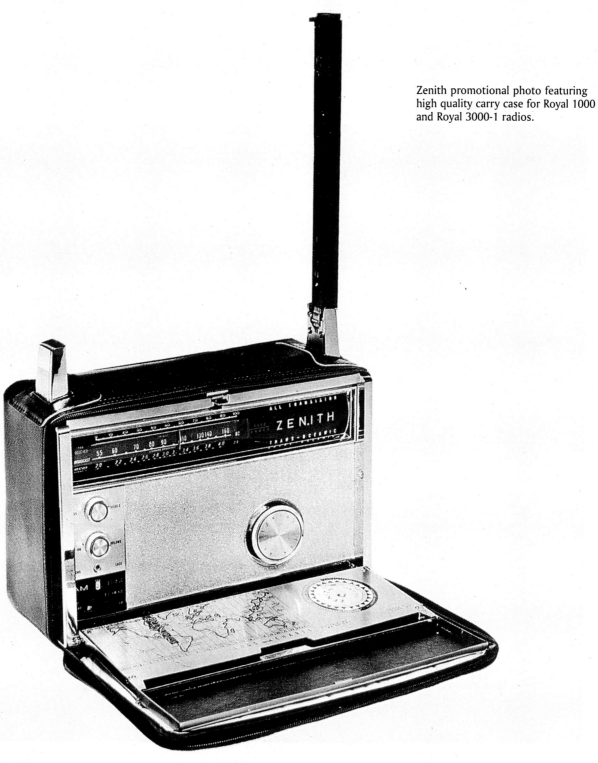

Zenith promotional photo featuring high quality carry case for Royal 1000 and Royal 3000-1 radios.

This luxurious new carry case is of rich looking, durable naugahyde in striking black color. Case is padded with foam rubber to provide extra protection for radio. Zippered front drops down to permit playing radio in case.

ORDER FROM YOUR ZENITH DISTRIBUTOR AS FORM No. R6124

FORM No. R6133-566

PRINTED IN U. S. A.

All New Carry Case For
Zenith Royal 7000 Trans-Oceanic Radio

RICH LOOKING!   FUNCTIONAL!

THIS HIGH QUALITY CARRY CASE IS COMPLETELY PADDED WITH FOAM RUBBER TO PROVIDE EXTRA PROTECTION FOR THE ROYAL 7000. THE CASE IS MADE OUT OF DURABLE NAUGAHYDE IN A STRIKING BLACK COLOR. FUNCTIONAL ZIPPERED POUCH DESIGNED TO HOLD RADIO LOG CHARTS AND HANDBOOKS. THE FRONT OF THE CARRY CASE DROPS DOWN TO PERMIT PLAYING RADIO IN CASE.

ORDER FROM YOUR ZENITH DISTRIBUTOR AS FORM No. R8318

FORM NO. R8324-1268   PRINTED IN U.S.A.

ZENITH PATENT DRAWINGS

Shown here are Zenith cabinet design patent draw-
ings from 1956, 1959, and 1961.

Patent drawing for Radio Receiver Cabinet, June 26, 1956.

Opposite page:
Zenith promotional photo featuring high quality carry
case for Royal 7000.

FIG.1

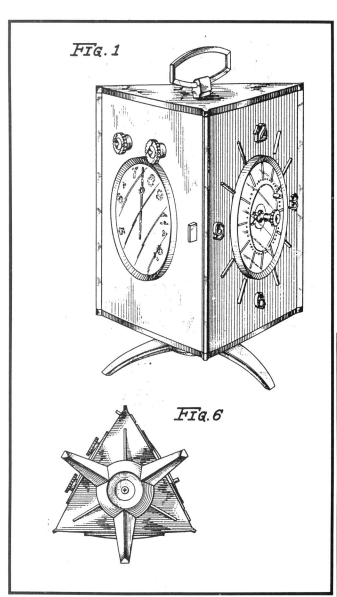

FIG.6

Des. 185,732
PAGE 2

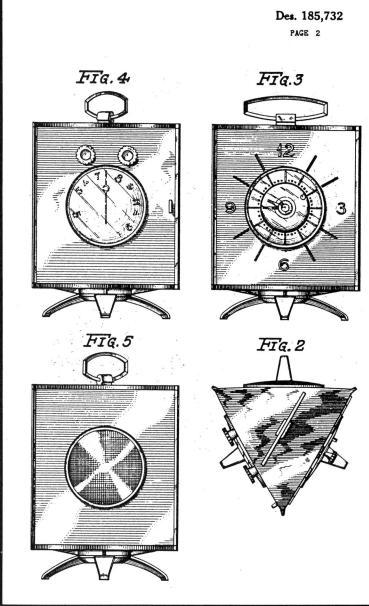

FIG.4 FIG.3

FIG.5 FIG.2

Patent drawing for Combined Clock
and Radio, July 28, 1959.

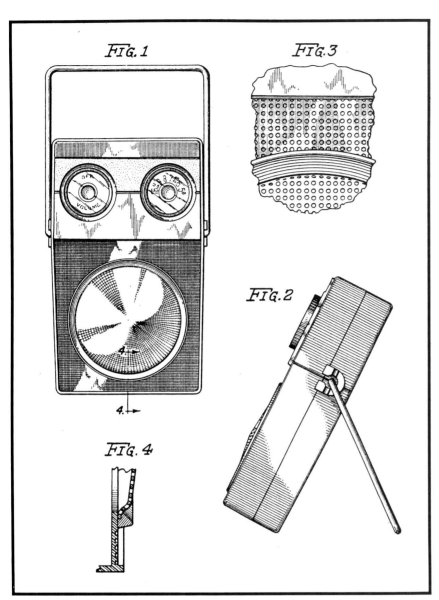

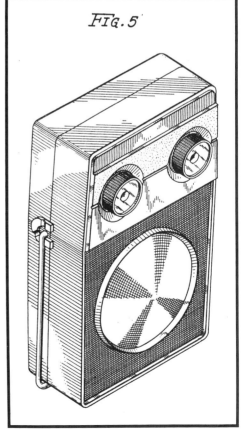

FIG.1 FIG.3 FIG.2 FIG.4 FIG.5

Patent drawing for Portable
Radio Cabinet, January 3, 1961.

155

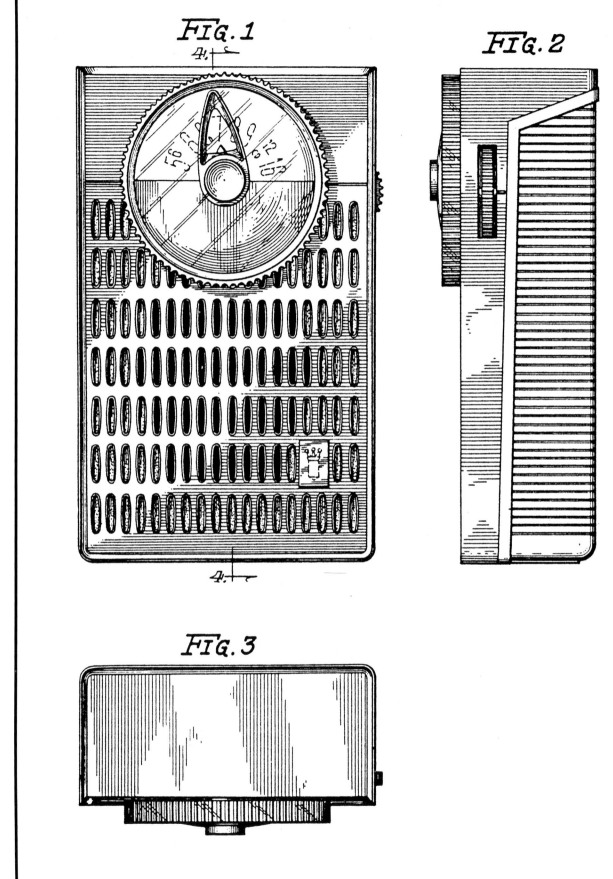

FIG.1

FIG.2

FIG.3

Front view: Patent drawing for Portable Radio Cabinet, April 4, 1961.

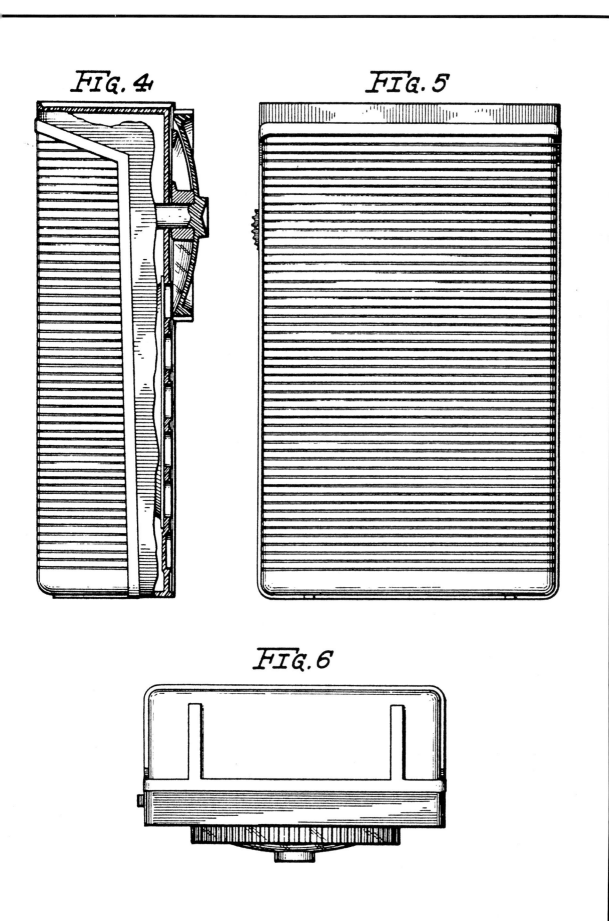

FIG. 4

FIG. 5

FIG. 6

Back view: Patent drawing for Portable Radio Cabinet, April 4, 1961.

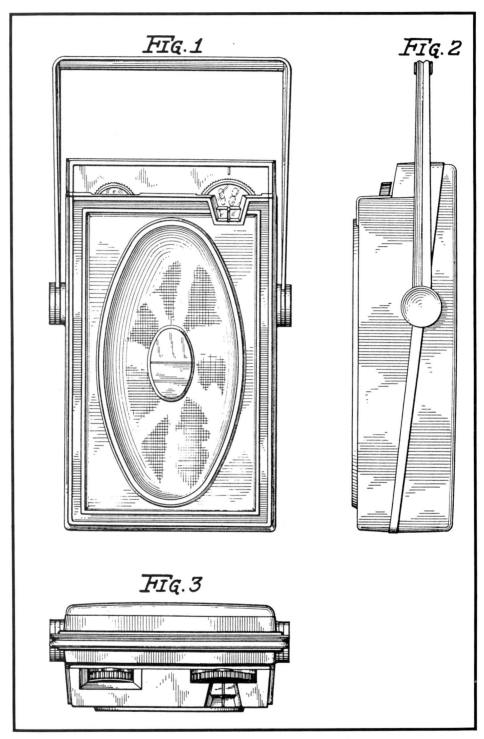

FIG.1

FIG.2

FIG.3

Front view: Patent drawing for Portable Radio Cabinet, October 17, 1961.

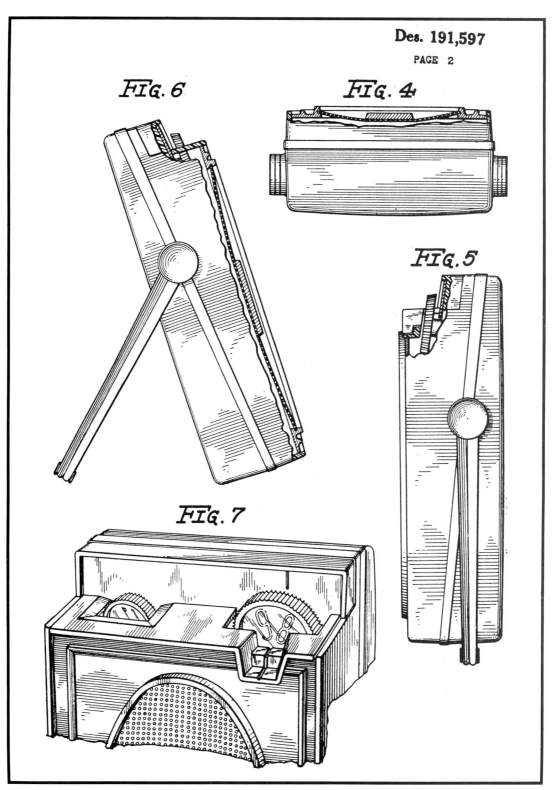

FIG. 6

FIG. 4

FIG. 5

FIG. 7

Side view: Patent drawing for Portable Radio Cabinet, October 17, 1961.

GLOSSARY

Amplifier. A circuit designed to increase the strength of weak signals.

Antenna, "Zenith Wave-Magnet." A system of conductors used to intercept radio signals.

Audio frequency. 20-20,000 cycles per second, the range of normal human hearing.

Audio output. The strength of a signal at audio frequencies.

Beat Frequency Oscillator (BFO). A circuit designed to allow reception of code and side-band signals.

Capacitor. A component consisting of conducting plates which are separated by an insulator. Some types have movable sections which enable use in tuned circuits.

Ceramic magnet technology. The use of a moldable magnetic material, which, when solidified, creates a compact, high strength magnet ideal for use in speakers.

Direct drive tuning. A form of tuning in which the tuning knob is attached directly onto the movable shaft of the tuning capacitor.

Direction finding. The use of a directional antenna and associated circuitry to determine the location of radio stations with relation to one's position.

Germanium diode. A device used to detect radio signals and to convert them for use in the audio amplifier.

Heterodyne. The result of combining signals of different frequencies in order to obtain a signal of new frequency. Either the sum or difference of the two is generally the desired resulting frequency.

Intermediate frequency. The heterodyne of beat frequency produced by the local oscillator and mixer, or converter stages in a super-heterodyne radio.

Milliwatt. A unit of energy, one thousandth of a watt.

Oscillator. Circuitry designed to generate A.C. at some desired frequency from a D.C. source.

Radio frequency. Those frequencies employed for the transmission of radio signals, ranging from 10 Khz through 100,000 Mhz.

Resonant point. The frequency which is mechanically natural for a given structure.

Vernier tuning. A system, usually ball bearing or gear driven, used for more precise control of the tuning capacitor in radio receivers.

Voice coil. The coil of wire wound around a form at the driving point of a loudspeaker.